Baja California

Baja California

EDITED BY

LISA AND SVEN-OLOF LINDBLAD

WITH CONTRIBUTIONS BY

DENNIS CORNEJO, GEORGE LINDSAY,

AND IAN McTAGGART-COWAN

RIZZOLI
NEW YORK

For George and Gerry Lindsay
in whose delightful company we came to
know and love Baja California

PHOTO CAPTIONS

Page 1: Fishermen, Sea of Cortez

Page 2: Rio Muleje

Pages 6–7: Brown pelicans

Pages 8–9: Bottlenose dolphins, Sea of Cortez

Pages 12–13: Batholith, Baja California's central desert

Front cover Isla Santa Catalina, Sea of Cortez
    (Photo by Sven-Olof Lindblad)
Back cover Cabo San Lucas (Photo by Sven-Olof Lindblad)

First published in the United States of America in 1987 by
RIZZOLI INTERNATIONAL PUBLICATIONS, INC.
597 Fifth Avenue, New York, NY 10017

Copyright © 1987 Rizzoli International Publications, Inc.
and Special Expeditions, Inc.

Library of Congress Cataloging-in-Publication Data
Baja California
   Bibliography: p.
   1. Baja California (Mexico)—Description and
travel—Views.   2. Natural history—Mexico—
Baja California—Pictorial works.   I. Lindblad,
Sven-Olof.   II. Lindblad, Lisa
F1246.B17   1987   917.2'2'00222   87–45491
ISBN 0–8478–0869–6
ISBN 0–8478–0872–6 (pbk.)

Book design by Gilda Hannah
Composition by Rainsford Type, Ridgefield, CT
Printed and bound in Japan

Contents

ACKNOWLEDGMENTS

We are grateful to Daniel Anderson of the University of California, Davis, Carlos Nagel of Cultural Exchange Services, and Albert Utton of the University of New Mexico for their generous contributions in the course of conversation; to Richard Ellis for reading portions of the manuscript and to Pamela Fingleton for her assistance.

The original map was created by Robert Trondsen.

Special thanks to Solveig Williams and Melissa Pierson of Rizzoli; and to Gilda Hannah for helping to shape this book.

PHOTOGRAPH CREDITS

Stewart Aitchison, p. 70 (middle left)
Tom Bean, p. 100
Peter Beck, pp. 60–61
Tui de Roy, pp. 92–93, 157 (lower)
François Gohier, pp. 6–7, 12–13, 16, 18, 31, 34 (lower right), 38, 44, 70 (upper right), 120–121, 134–135, 156, 158, 172–173, 174, 175, 179
Howard Hall, pp. 42, 58, 59, 64, 65, 70 (middle right, lower left and right), 71, 75 (lower), 76, 77, 160, 166–167, 176, 177, 180–181
Enrique Hambleton, pp. 2, 24–25, 74, 78–79, 112, 130, 131, 132, 133, 142–143
Gary James, pp. 32, 148–149, 171
Dotte Larsen, pp. 56–57
Bud Lehnhausen, pp. 52, 84–85, 146, 152–153, 155 (lower)
Sven-Olof Lindblad, pp. 20–21, 26, 27, 39, 40–41, 46–47, 50–51, 53, 62–63, 68–69, 95 (middle left and right), 96–97, 98–99, 106, 108, 110–111, 116–117, 126, 127, 128–129, 155 (upper), 157 (upper), 169, 182
George Lindsay, p. 34 (lower left)
C. Allan Morgan, pp. 54–55, 66–67, 70 (upper left), 75 (upper), 95 (upper and lower right), 101, 104–105, 124, 125, 136–137, 140–141, 144, 170
Kevin Schafer, pp. 8–9, 28–29, 30, 33, 34 (upper right), 35, 36–37, 80, 82, 88–89, 95 (lower left), 102, 107, 109, 139, 162–163
James C. Simmons, pp. 23, 114, 138
Jeremiah S. Sullivan, pp. 1, 34 (upper left), 72–73, 95 (upper left), 103
Soames Summerhays, p. 178

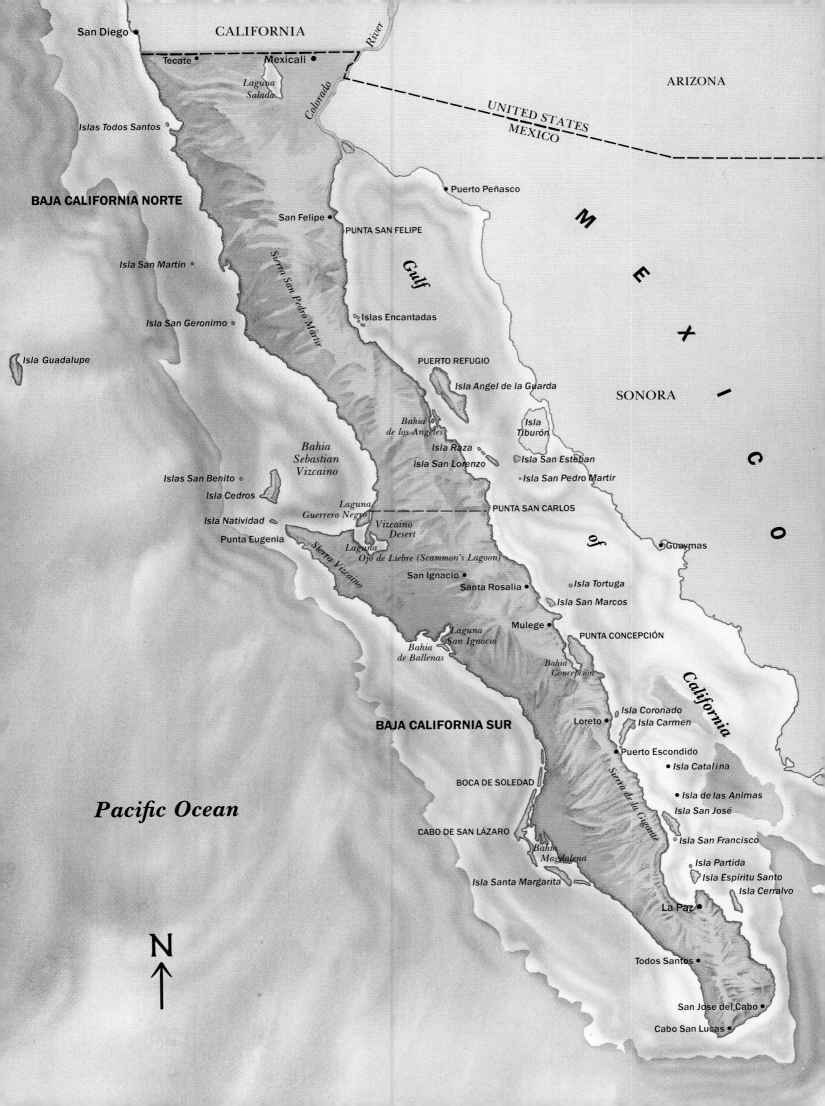

Introduction

Baja California extends southward like a gnarled finger for eight hundred miles from the United States border of California. It is a strangely beautiful wilderness steeped in mystery. Surrounded by two seas of extraordinary richness, this realm of land and water is replete with parched mountainscapes, bizarre plants, whales, and isolated islands teeming with sea birds and animals.

Until recently, only avid fishermen, a few scientists, and the odd adventurer have journeyed to this little known paradise. For the rest, mention of Baja California may bring to mind the Baja 1000, that most grueling car race, and Mexican border towns, such as Mexicali and Tijuana, which offer cheap booze and a good time. In 1973, the government built Mexico Highway 1 down the length of the peninsula, enabling visitors to make the trip from border to cape in three comfortable days instead of a bone-rattling ten. And the tourists have responded, coming in increasing numbers to fish and soak up the sun at any one of the numerous resorts spread along the coast of the cape region.

There is a world beyond the border towns and the Mexican "Riviera," however, that is still virtually untrod, largely due to geographical inaccessibility. The enigmatic cave paintings tucked away in the sierras can be reached only after arduous pack-mule travel and then some hiking. Boats are needed to explore the whale lagoons. You have to hike through cracked, rock-strewn arroyos to find their hidden life and through desert forests to see the infinitely varied boojums that coil their spindly limbs in whiplike arcs. It almost seems as if life flourishes here with such abandon because of the land's inhospitality to man.

Sun and heat have baked the earth hard as unglazed clay, and it takes special sight, "desert eyes," to discover the land's beauty, finding in the haze of pale yellows and mauves the pinprick crimson of a flower, the yellow flash of a hummingbird's throat, the backlit halo of a barrel cactus's spines. Subtle beauty is the essence of Baja California's appeal and it takes time and sensitivity to appreciate it.

I was a relative latecomer to Baja California when I boarded an airplane for Bahía de los Angeles six years ago. I had heard the superlatives often—Mexico's Galapagos, the richest sea in the world, the rejuvenating magic of the Gulf—but, on arrival, I saw a landscape that looked as if it were dying from thirst. Friable, rocky sand made walking tricky and the plants, if they had any embellishment at all, wore an armor of spines. It seemed a desolate world, and I thought it dreary.

It wasn't until I reached Isla San Marcos in the Sea of Cortéz that I remember seeing vivid color. A sally lightfoot crab scuttled over a tidepool rock and those red legs delighted me. My eyes began to adjust to the desert's muted palette. Walking up a sandy wash, the air steeped in sun-impregnated herbal smells, I found a bush with clouds of tiny white blossoms. The frenzied movement of a hummingbird drew me to the waxy white flower of a cardon cactus. The smooth skin of the cactus stalk stretched in ridges and grooves that ran like railroad tracks, converging at a faraway point in the blue sky.

I was completely enchanted when, one day aboard ship, I heard the cry "Whale to port!" I looked down into the clear water onto a back as smooth as polished ebony. A finback whale, the second largest mammal ever to inhabit the earth, had joined us and, surfacing with an easy rhythm, he followed our bow for an hour or more. Close enough to be misted by his blow, I watched spellbound as his lithe body navigated the water like a true thoroughbred.

One late afternoon at Isla San Pedro Mártir, my husband and I waited in a skiff for the sun to set. Sea lions were still cavorting in the waning light, sending bubbles up around our boat and, occasionally, coming up for a look at us with their soup-plate eyes. Boobies were ferrying urgently back and forth between the large island and offshore rocks. The disk of the sun turned deep red and began to slip below the horizon. Suddenly, it felt cold; whistles, squawks, and bellows echoed in the thinning air. Dark comes quickly in the Gulf and we readied ourselves to return to the ship. Rising out of the east, a full moon balanced the setting sun for a moment and then took possession of the sky, climbing rapidly and gaining strength. The sea lions had hauled out on rocky landings by now, but the black shadows of frigate birds and boobies wheeled overhead and, occasionally, like witches on broomsticks, crossed the band of moonlight inching toward the island's white cliffs.

Ultimately, what I find most compelling about Baja California and the Sea of Cortéz is the busyness of life. Few places exist today where nature proceeds so unhindered with its own agenda. There is something primeval about the area, a feeling that the environment is settled and used according to an original design; that you are a witness to what has always been.

But, as with any paradise today, its safety and integrity must consciously be maintained. Recognizing this, Mexico declared forty-seven islands in the Sea of Cortéz wildlife refuges in 1978. While this status entails little infrastructural support, the proclamation alerted Mexicans and the world to the presence of a truly extraordinary heritage. The Government's determination to protect Baja California's natural refuges has meant reevaluating a host of threats to the area.

One major threat is the drying up of the Colorado River, the most controlled and intensively used river in the United States, and what that means to the Sea of Cortéz. Before its extensive damming, the Colorado had the greatest silt load of any river in the world. That nutrient-laden silt has been deposited for the last ten to fourteen million years in a large delta area extending to the head of the Gulf of California. Today, unless water flow is unusually great, the Colorado River is reduced to a trickle by the time it reaches the Gulf. The delta spawning grounds of fish such as the totuava have been destroyed. The broader effects are still being studied.

Overfishing, and certain fishing techniques, are also cause for concern. Gill netting is particularly disastrous, trapping sea lions, dolphins, pilot whales, and some sea birds along with the catch. Frequent deep neck slashes on sea lions attest to the awful damage this method can cause. Overfishing of anchovies, sardines, and shrimp has not only drastically reduced those resources but also endangers the ecosystem's overall health by disrupting important links in the food chain.

Tourism, as is so often the case, is a mixed blessing. The fragility of the environment, coupled with the current lack of manpower to control human movement, makes the issue particularly timely. The challenge is to make Baja California's rich natural life an economic and political asset for Mexico without, in the process, destroying it. Tourism, while making this possible, must also provide the capital to preserve the wildlife. Scientific studies, the cooperation of conservation organizations and tour operators, and the sensitivity of understanding tourists could enable Baja California to become an excellent model of resource management, and ensure its survival as a fascinating destination for the nature lover.

Baja California has demonstrated a centuries-old, stubborn resistance to the encroachments of man. This "waterless thornfull rock, sticking up between two oceans," as it was described by a missionary in 1752, has repulsed most efforts to gentle its contours, to extract its riches. It has survived wonderfully intact for centuries, a secret wilderness on a very crowded planet. May it continue to thrive.

LISA LINDBLAD

A Desert

Garden

Viewed from a distance, perhaps from an airplane or a ship, Baja California may appear stark and severe. It is, with the exception of high mountains at either end, a desert. Deserts are not clothed in dense vegetation, green forests, and velvet grasslands. Yet the conditions of aridity and isolation in Baja California seem to have been ideal for the development of many remarkable plants, some bizarre, others grotesque, all of them fantastic. Baja California is in fact a desert garden of startling beauty.

The Baja California peninsula is part of the Sonora Desert which extends up into Arizona and down the western coast of the Mexican mainland to the Rio Mayo. The Sonora Desert flora is rich and useful. Of the 2,500 vascular plants in this desert, there are over 425 wild edible species and roughly 25 crop species that have been cultivated since prehistoric times.[1]

Life originated in water and water remains the absolute essential for life. Land plants and animals are really canteens, preserving their primal aquatic environment within themselves. Since deserts lack water and the conditions of high temperatures, together with extreme light intensity, and rapid evaporation create a hostile environment, only highly modified and adapted organisms can survive in them.

Strategems for water conservation are responsible for the bizarre and beautiful plants of Baja California. Morphological modifications, combined with less conspicuous physiological adaptations, have prepared the plants to meet the challenge of survival in an arid area. Some develop water-storage tissue; these include the cacti, century plants, ice plants, yuccas, elephant trees, copals, and many others, all called *succulents*. Some have tremendous root systems which probe the depths to suck up moisture. Botanist Forrest Shreve once remarked that if the desert were turned inside out, it would show itself to be abundant in vegetation, because the root development of xerophytes is so much more extensive than the aerial portions of the plants.[2] Nearly all succulents are protected from herbivores by spines or thorns, or by distasteful or dangerous chemicals in their juices. Other plants survive the normally long drought periods just by remaining tough-coated seeds, only germinating when the soil is moistened by the brief rains. Sometimes called *ephemeral* because they last such a short time, they may germinate, grow, bloom, and set seed again in only a few weeks.

To the visitor of Baja California, the most ubiquitous floral elements are the spine-covered cacti, which have been called "the truculent succulents." There are more than 120 kinds of cacti growing on the peninsula and its adjacent islands. Seventy of them are endemic, occurring nowhere else. Some of them are quite tiny, smaller than one's thumb. Cardons, or giant cacti, form open forests of towering, fluted stems which bristle with protective thorns. I once measured a giant among the giants a few miles inland from Bahía des los Angeles in a spectacular cardon forest. It was sixty-four feet tall and I estimated its weight at twelve

Page 16: Desert in bloom
Page 18: Lichens, Isla San Benitos

tons. Imagine this forest in March and April when the cardons bear masses of white flowers on the south sides of their upper branches, followed by golden fruits which split to reveal red flesh. The flowers are pollinated by hummingbirds, bats, and hawk moths. The fruit attracts mourning doves and white-winged doves and a host of other birds.

While walking in Baja California care must be taken to avoid the vicious spines and easily detached joints of the jumping chollas which seem to spring at the passerby and impale themselves in the calf. This is the plant's method of reproduction, the joint being carried away to strike roots and grow in a new place. Other cacti are the barrels, voluptuous even with their spiny armor, the little nipple cacti, and the luscious fruit-bearing organ-pipe or sweet pitahaya cacti which were of enormous importance to the indigenous peoples of Baja California.

Organ-pipe cacti provide food and wine for any number of species. Long-nosed frugivorous bats hover over the funnel-shaped flowers of the pitahaya dulce, as it is called in Mexico, lapping the nectar. Noctuid moths move in through the openings left by the bats and drink frenziedly. Desert pallid bats, quintessential insectivores, block the openings and eat the moths, gaining some nutrients from the pitahaya syrup as well. In the heat of day, fermentation occurs and the still-open blossoms draw swarms of fruitflies and bees to their pools of nectar. They drink until drunk, then fall in, and drown.

The fruit of the pitahaya dulce has enticed the human animal as well, and has been served on the tables of Baja Californians for centuries. Miguel del Barco, an eighteenth-century priest in the Loreto area, opined that ''All of them are excellent fruit, worthy of being on the table of the greatest of kings.''[3] The Jesuit missionaries noted that, during the heavy crop of the summer, the hungry Indians wandered the hills eating until they could eat no more, sleeping a few hours, to rise and eat again.[4] Today the pitahaya is still an important and popular fruit which can be eaten fresh, made into sweet preserves, or even mashed and fermented to produce a mild cactus wine.

As succulents, the cardons, pitahayas, and barrel cacti have ridges and grooves, like the bellows of an accordion, which permit them to expand rapidly to absorb water. The water is retained by a waxy, waterproof skin and complex physiological modifications. Cacti are leafless and photosynthesis is accomplished in their green stems. The ability to retain water of some cacti is astonishing. One barrel cactus, in shaded laboratory conditions, lived and flowered five years with no water at all.

Leaves are prodigal with water, and those of desert plants are usually reduced to small leathery organs coated with waterproof waxes or fine hairs or even modified into protective spines. Some desert plants do have larger and more typical leaves but these are deciduous, appearing briefly for food manufacture after a rain, only to drop when soil moisture is depleted.

If our desert walk takes us into central Baja California, we see that the most conspicuous plant is the cirio, or boojum, tree, one of the strangest in the world. Boojums are weird-looking trees, with tapering trunks fifteen to fifty feet tall. The Mexican name ''cirio'' comes from their resemblance to the tall wax tapers used in the mission churches. From a base eighteen inches to two feet thick, the trunk rises with an ever decreasing diameter, to be topped with a little plume of white flowers. Some of the trunks divide into thick, often twisting limbs, and all have short leaf-bearing branchlets. In times of drought the plants are leafless and protected from dessication by thick, waxy epidermal layers. With the next rains, a little cluster of leaves bursts from the base of each spine. The new leaves are fully expanded within seventy-two hours and the plant is photosynthesizing at full capacity, taking advantage of the brief availability of water. Many other desert plants, particularly shrubs and trees, take advantage of their food-manufacturing leaves when moisture is available and shed them to avoid the danger of large evaporative surfaces when water is gone.

Occurring with boojums in the extremely arid midpeninsula, and making that area a wonderland of plant monstrosities, is the elephant tree. Usually

Pages 20–21: Cardon cacti, Isla San Pedro Mártir

thick-trunked, gnarled, and only ten to twelve feet tall, in favorable localities they may grow much larger. On rocky ridges elephant trees are often dwarfed and contorted into beautiful natural bonsais. Near the Pacific Ocean elephant trees are wind-trained, their corpulent trunks sprawling along the ground much as those of conifers at timberline. The thick trunks bear several ponderous limbs which twist and bend in an astonishing fashion, then terminate in a few dry, brittle twigs that bear tiny leaves which occur briefly after rains. A paper-thin, yellow epidermal layer peels and shreds to reveal the blue-green, waxy-smooth covering of the inner bark, which is quite spongy and has a milky juice which dries into a translucent gum. The bark is used by ranchers for tanning leather. Cream, pink, or red tiny flowers appear on the spineless, leafless trees during the hottest summer months, in such great quantities as to give the whole landscape a light, fairyland appearance. With no spines for defense, the elephant tree has developed an astringent sap, distasteful and poisonous to herbivores.

In the glorious cardon forest behind Bahía de los Angeles, one cannot help but be delighted with the diversity of vegetation within view. Unlike the monotonous northern forests, the Baja California desert parades plants of great variety. Palo verde, ironwood, and mesquite trees, creosote bushes, succulent century plants, joshua trees, and many others share the sandy bed with the boojums, chollas, pitahayuas, and cardons. To this array is added, on rare occasions, a blanket of annual wildflowers which, when conditions are right, sets the whole land ablaze with the most vivid colors packaged in the tiniest blossoms imaginable. Lasting less than a month and occurring every three or four years, Baja California deserts become a magical flower garden.

When the rains have bypassed the peninsula for a year of two, it might be hard for the visitor to recognize the beauty and magic of this land at first. The colors seem monotone, the plants, inhospitable. It takes but a few days, however, to appreciate the washed shades of mauves and greens that tint the landscape and give it definition, to recognize an unusual kind of beauty in the twisted shape of an elephant tree, in the ridged skin of a cardon, in a cactus spine shedding its sheath. The magic of the desert lies in its potential to transform itself with vivid color, to burst forth with fruits that nourish birds, insects, and mammals. It is the beauty of form welded to function.

Desert plants are perfectly tuned to the constraints and the opportunities of their environment. They know when to be patient. The bloom of a cardon is gorgeous not only because of its color and fullness, but is especially beautiful because so much time and care and saving went into its making. When the rains come the desert blooms, becoming a fantasy land. At other times, the desert remains a garden of form and endless possibility.

GEORGE LINDSAY

NOTES
1. Gary Paul Nabhan, *Gathering The Desert* (Tucson: University of Arizona Press, 1985), p. 6.
2. Personal communication with the author.
3. Nabhan, *Gathering the Desert*, p. 82.
4. Johann Jakob Baegert, *Observations in Lower California*, translated from the German with introduction and notes by M. M. Brandenburg and Carl L. Baumann (Berkeley: University of California Press, 1952), p. 35.

Page 23: Agave plant, Isla Cedros
Pages 24–25: Sierra de la Laguna

Page 26: Giant barrel cactus, Isla Catalina
Page 27: Boojum trees and cardon cacti, Montevideo canyon
Pages 28–29: Boojum tree and granite boulders, Cataviña

26

Page 30: Boojum trees
Page 31: Red-tailed hawk nesting in a boojum tree

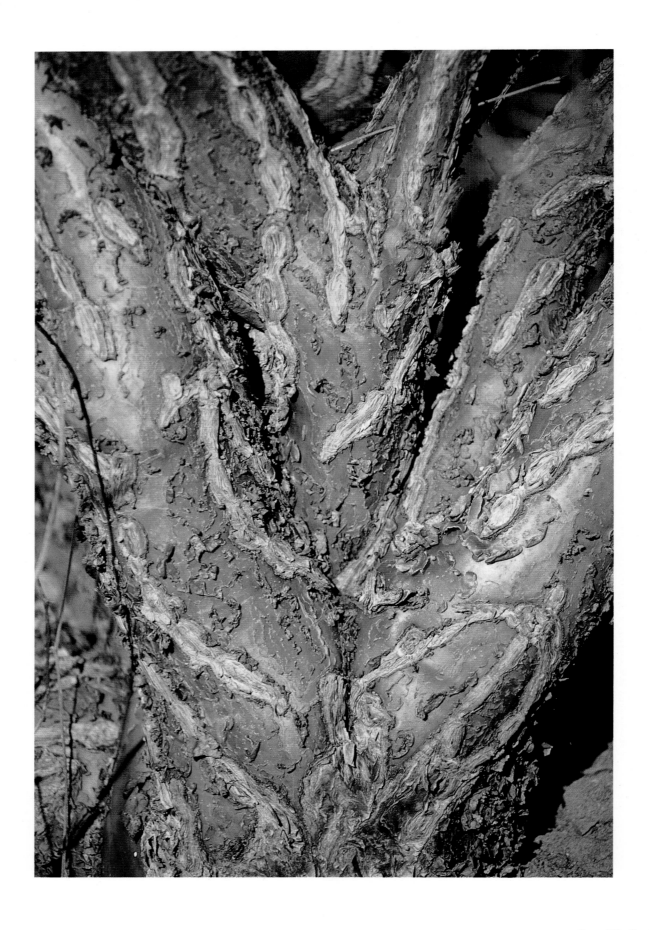

Page 32: *Ocotillo bark*
Page 33: *Elephant tree*

Page 34: Upper left, Prickly pear cactus; upper right,
Cochemia cactus; lower left, Pincussion cactus growing near
northwestern beach; lower right, Iceplant

Page 35: Prickly pear cactus

The Sea
of Cortez

The Sea of Cortez fills the gigantic cleft separating Baja California from the Mexican mainland. The great movements that tore the peninsula from the continent occurred some four and a half million years ago and, ever since, this sliver of land has moved northwestward with time, spreading and deepening the trench. The adventurous conquistador Hernándo Cortéz sailed up the gulf in 1535. Although his name has become poetically linked to the sea, its correct appellation is the Gulf of California.

Today the Gulf stretches seven hundred miles in length. It opens broadly onto the Pacific Ocean at its entrance, squeezes to a width of only thirty miles at the point where Tiburón Island now lies against the Mexican coast, and then expands again at its head.

Oceanographers identify four major regions within the Gulf.[1] The northern portion, between the Colorado River delta and the midriff islands, received the silts from that river for millions of years until the Hoover Dam, constructed in 1935, cut off the flow of nutrients. The silt has rounded the bottom contours and lies as much as three miles deep in the trench. The water here has a greater seasonal temperature fluctuation than anywhere else in the Gulf. It is turbid, highly saline, and has tidal ranges of up to twenty-eight feet. These factors combine to make it a region of special planktonic richness. It teams with phytoplankton and zooplankton and the larvae and young stages of many fishes.

The midriff island area is unique. Fierce currents scour basins up to 2,700 feet deep, producing high bottom temperatures, salinity, and oxygen levels. Biological productivity is high.

The central portion, from the midriff islands south to La Paz, features very deep basins, little silting, and little tidal rise and fall. Upwelling occurs in the lee of many islands, bringing nutrients to the surface waters.

The southern portion, below La Paz, is oceanic in nature. It has very steep slopes and submarine canyons plunging to twelve thousand feet below the sea's surface.

Thus there is remarkable variety in the Sea of Cortez. The transition from heavily silted, shallow depths with extreme seasonal changes in water temperature and salinity to great depths in clear, unsilted water where moderate conditions prevail is dramatic. In between, there are regions of fierce currents, turbulence, and constant renewal. With such a range in conditions, it is not surprising that the Sea of Cortez's biological diversity and abundance is unequaled in other regions of similar size.

The base of all food pyramids is phytoplankton, primarily diatoms and dinoflagellates, the microscopic plants that are the builders of organic material. Grazing on them are a great assortment of zooplankton creatures, from protozoa to crustaceans, and the larvae of many larger invertebrates and fishes. Farther along the web are the many creatures, mostly carnivores, that swim freely, predating and being preyed upon. Sharks, large fishes, many sea birds, toothed whales, and sea lions cap the food pyramid.

It is the plankton swarms that fire the "engine"

Page 42: California sea lions
Page 44: Yellow spotted starfish

of the Sea of Cortez. Their numbers, variety, and awesome capacity to multiply provide the fuel that enables the flamboyant manifestations of life which are the hallmark of these waters. A close look at the shoreline suggests that every niche is occupied. Soft mud, sandy mud, surf-pounded sand, mangrove trunks, cobble bottoms, boulders, cliff faces, dead shells, even the cavities within sponges—each supports creatures living off the plankton, off the organic detritus, off each other's larvae, or off each other.

More than eight hundred species of fish have been catalogued in the Gulf and more are added with each serious study of the area. Almost half of them are reef fish.[2]

The rocky shores from Cabo San Lucas to the southern midriff islands provide a feast for the eyes of the snorkeler or diver: schools of sergeant majors, five vertical black stripes on their silver and yellow bodies; king angelfish in striking patterns of brown, orange, and blue; moorish idols with white streamers from their yellow and black dorsal fins; and azure parrotfish are but a few of the denizens of these waters. But it is the schooling fishes of the Gulf that testify to its biological richness.

Sardines, anchovies, thread herrings, flatiron herrings, and grunions are among the plankton feeders present in vast schools in the open sea. Millions of these small fish are pursued by the predatory species. Schools, acres in area, of needlefish, half-beak, machete barracuda, and bonito are frequent. Ray Cannon writes about seeing a ten-mile-long horde of game fish feeding on a still larger body of forage fish, a meal which produced a fish pileup. Large schools of yellowtail, bonito, and skipjack tore into even larger hordes of sardine, herring, and other small fishes. These took to the air in such numbers as to form "a solid silver blanket two to three feet above the surface . . . that spread in all directions for a hundred yards or so." It is under such conditions, he goes on to report, "that every fish-eating creature of the Sea dashes into the fray . . . [and] the normally calm, limpid face of the sea is churned into convulsions of mass slaughter."[3] Birds, from pelicans and terns to cormorants, stream in from all directions, plunging and diving between the leaping forms of dolphins, all thrashing about in a feeding frenzy.

The concentrations of big fish attracted to the abundant food is wondrous. Black marlin, striped marlin, sailfish, wahoo, dolphin fish, and sharks are widely distributed and numerous.

Not all the large fish are carnivores. One memorable February morning a huge shoal of manta rays cruised slowly along in a glassy sea, fin-wings undulating and feeding palps widespread to direct plankton into their open mouths. A single thirty-foot whale shark, also a plankton feeder, glided along in their midst.

Birds, too, have responded to the felicitous combination of abundant food and ideal nesting environments. Brown pelicans, brown boobies, blue-footed boobies, and Heermann's gulls are the day-hunting species found in large numbers.

Marine scientist Daniel Anderson says, "The Gulf of California offers a paradoxical environment for those organisms that would invade its waters and flourish. On one hand it has some of the greatest environmental extremes of any of the world's seas. . . . Counterposed against these conditions is the great productivity of the Gulf . . . with its abundance of life at higher levels of the food web. A mobile sea bird is an ideally suited vertebrate for this environment, for it can migrate or disperse to avoid harsh conditions yet it can move into such an area to take advantage of the abundant resources."[4]

Fifteen species of marine birds nest within the Sea of Cortez area. Many of them move on, once their young are independent, to range over the Pacific Ocean north and south of Cabo San Lucas.

The nesting sea bird populations are phenomenal. With half a million pairs, the least storm-petrel exceeds all others. The Heermann's gull, the brown pelican, elegant tern, and eleven other species total 336,000 pairs. They nest on some fifteen islands and islets. In general, the smaller and more isolated the islet, the greater attraction it has for sea birds. Each species' slightly different needs for nesting conditions keeps competition at a minimum.

Tiny Isla Raza, only a few miles from Isla San

Pages 46–47: Feeding dolphins in the Sea of Cortez

Pedro Mártir, is one of these attractive spots. Just over half a square kilometer, this flat, stony island lures the majority of the world's population of Heermann's gulls in early March of each year. Virtually a platform of birds, estimates of the number of gulls on the island and in dense flocks on the surrounding sea have been as high as 310,000; the clamor is deafening. The densest concentration of nests occurs in a saucerlike depression near the middle of the island where the ground is relatively sandy. Their nests are spaced about sixteen inches apart, the minimum distance that aggression will allow. A large colony of royal and elegant terns surrounds and hems in the gulls. This is living dangerously at its most dramatic as the Heermann's gull is an aggressive nest predator. Somehow a state of dynamic equilibrium is achieved by the three species.

Raza, like San Pedro Mártir, was subject to guano mining. By 1880, it was reported that ten thousand tons of guano had been removed from the island and that sixty thousand tons remained.

Guano mining was not as deleterious to the bird colonies of Raza as was commercial egg collecting which began about the turn of the century and continued for almost sixty years. By the 1950s there was a serious decline in bird population and some of the former nesting sites of Heermann's gulls had already been abandoned. In 1964 Mexico responded to this threatening situation by creating a National Reserve and Refuge for Migratory Birds on the island.[5]

The California sea lion is the only pinniped in the Sea of Cortez. It is a roamer, frequently seen far at sea as it moves from one to another of the favored rookeries and haul-out sites such as Los Islotes, San Pedro Mártir, Angel de la Guarda, and San Lorenzo. It is impossible to recall these remote and beautiful places without remembering the bedlam that accompanies any group of these creatures. The graceful porpoising of yearlings drawn to your boat by an insatiable curiosity, the great black bulls, and the pale brown cows and their young, draped in total relaxation over the most uncomfortable-looking rocks, the pervasive odor of recycled fish, the incessant accompaniment of

barks, bellows, belches, and yelps—all this is part of the sea lion world.

Knowledge of the whales and dolphins of the Gulf is growing as a result of studies being undertaken by the Department of Fisheries of Baja California and by biologists from California. Even when unmolested the great whales do not occur in large numbers in the world's oceans. Today, after decades of merciless slaughter, they are scarcer than ever before. Even so there are areas, scattered about the oceans, where one can usually find one or more species. The Gulf of California is one of these. It is not unusual to encounter six or more species of whales here during a week at sea. Thirteen species have been recorded. One of these, the Gulf porpoise *Phocoena sinus*, is found nowhere else and is among the rarest of cetaceans.

Seldom does a day go by in the Gulf without a company of bottle-nosed or common dolphin visiting your ship. The latter, especially, seem to enjoy streaking toward the ship from half a mile or more away to play in the bow pressure-wave.

In late spring small pods of shortfin pilot whales can be met in the area between Isla Espíritu Santo and Isla Danzante.

Occasionally in late spring small groups of sperm whales have been seen in the same area, always over the deepest parts of the trench where they hunt large squid and deep ocean fishes, detected by echolocation in the blackness of the ocean depths. Orcas are infrequently seen, probably because their numbers are small and they are constantly on the move, ranging over the entire Gulf.

The baleen whales are the most spectacular of the cetaceans here, and are sufficiently numerous that one expects to encounter them in the course of two or three days at sea. Canal de Ballenas, as its name implies, is an area of concentration for the four species of rorquals. The gigantic finback is the most numerous and is present year-round, as is the similar but smaller Bryde's whale. The giant among whales, the blue whale, appears in late spring and seems to be slowly increasing in numbers. The Minke whale, smallest of these rorqual or "pleated" whales, is rather scarce in the Gulf.

In my eight weeks of whale watching in the Sea

of Cortez, over a span five years, I have encountered only four humpback whales and four gray whales. The grays, formerly abundant in the southern area and the larger lagoons of the Sonora coast, are gradually reoccupying this part of their range as adventurers from the Pacific lagoons turn the corner at Cabo San Lucas.

The feeding strategies of the whales illustrate the diversity of their needs and the ability of the Gulf's waters to provide for them in abundance. Finbacks and blue whales are plankton feeders, Bryde's whales draw on schools of small fish, and humpbacks are consumers of both fish and plankton. The gray whale is possibly not feeding at all while it is in these southern waters. The toothed whales are pursuit predators, catching larger prey individually—the deep divers seeking squid and the shallower divers, fish.

One of the most spectacular feeding techniques of the baleen whales is lunge feeding. One day, while floating quietly on a glassy sea, we were surrounded by twelve finbacks, three blues, and a humpback. The great mammals arched up and disappeared smoothly, only to surge up from the depths a few minutes later, mouths and throats distended by the hundreds of gallons of water and prey engulfed. As they surfaced, they rolled onto their right sides, water gushing from the baleen filter. Three or four respirations on the surface prepared them to repeat the feeding process.

Perhaps the strangest creature using the resources of the Gulf is a fish-eating bat, *Pizonyx*. Confined to just a few islands, it is best known on Isla Partida Norte. It, too, is a specialist predator, hooking small fish from the surface of the sea with the long, curved, sharp claws of its hind feet.

Even the sea-going reptiles have found niches in the complex food web of the Sea of Cortez. In earlier times sea turtles were locally abundant. Despite a century of killing, three species, perhaps four, still occur in small numbers and one can occasionally see the odd individual, sometimes with a gull as passenger, floating on the surface.

There is only one species of sea snake along the Pacific coast of the Americas, the yellow-bellied sea snake, with its striking brown and orange markings. It reaches a maximum length of three feet, but northern specimens seldom exceed two feet. It feeds on fish employing a quite clever strategy. Since small fishes have an attachment to floating objects such as sticks and cluster close to them, this sea snake, just by floating quietly, has its meal delivered.

As a visitor to the Sea of Cortez one gains the impression that the ecosystem is complete and closely integrated, with few vacant niches and the biotic potential fully used. The wealth of the Sea of Cortez is, indeed, phenomenal and it comes from that particular mix of properties which produce the great plankton swarms of the Gulf. This is the fundamental link in the food chain, the base upon which all oceanic and terrestrial life in the Sea of Cortez builds. The sea, however, faces certain threats. It is too early to measure the long-term influence of the Hoover Dam on the nutrient cycle of the Gulf, but early data indicate serious repercussions. Neither are the data available to project the possible consequences of man's fishing on sea lion and bird populations. With increased human population there is always some environmental degradation. How much and where the problems lie are issues being addressed by joint teams of scientists from Mexico and the United States. For them, and increasingly for others, the Sea of Cortez is a resource to be understood and safeguarded.

IAN McTAGGART-COWAN

NOTES

1. L. Y. Maluf, "Physical Oceanography," in *Island Biogeography of the Sea of Cortez*, T. J. Case and M. L. Cody, eds. (Berkeley: University of California Press, 1983), pp. 26–43.

2. D. A. Thompson, L. T. Findley and A. N. Kerstish, *Reef Fish of the Sea of Cortez*, (New York: John Wiley, 1979).

3. R. Cannon, *The Sea of Cortez*, (Menlo Park, Cal.: Lane Magazine and Book Company, 1966), p. 91.

4. D. Anderson, "The Sea Birds," in *Island Biogeography in the Sea of Cortez*, pp. 246–64.

5. C. Bahre, "Human Impact: The Midriff Islands," in *Island Biogeography in the Sea of Cortez*, pp. 290–306.

Pages 50–51: California sea lions

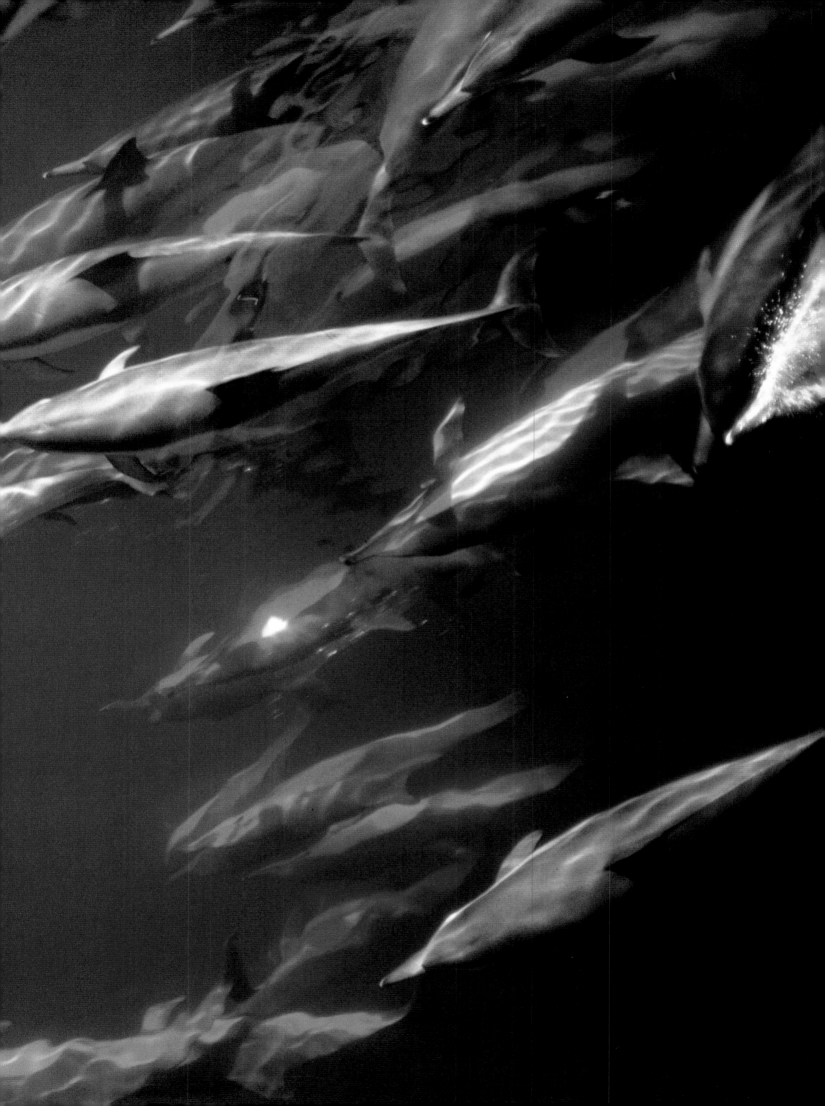

Page 58: Gorgonian coral
Page 59: Manta ray
Pages 60–61: Brown booby
Pages 62–63: Fishing fleet, Puerta Peñasco

Page 70: upper left, Sally lightfoot crab; upper right, Slate pencil urchin; middle left, Pacific ridley turtle; middle right, Scorpionfish; lower left, Spotted puffer; lower right, Nudibranch

Page 71: upper left, Starfish; upper right, Moray eel; middle left, Cortez angel fish; middle right, Flat worm; lower left, California spiny lobster; lower right, Gorgonian coral

Pages 72–73: Hammerhead sharks
Page 74: Sunset, Sea of Cortez
Page 75: Upper, Robust Gorgonian coral; lower, Guinea
fowl puffer

Page 76: Scorpionfish

Page 77: Gorgonian coral
Pages 78–79: San Juan de la Costa, Sea of Cortez

The
Enchanted
Islands

Wisps of hot vapor rose from the new black lava. Even though it was midday, the smoking mountain nearby was almost invisible, hidden by an atmosphere thick with ash. The new land was still virgin. It had never experienced the miracle of a seed rooting deep into its crust. No bird had ever sung here to a rising sun. No two creatures had yet joined to reproduce, and colonize this barren landscape. It would still be many years before the first plants would grow or the first animals would arrive, but the story of the islands of the Sea of Cortez begins with the rock from which they were formed.[1]

The most important geological feature of the Sea of Cortez (Gulf of California) is the major strike-slip fault which underlies the Gulf. Such a fault is created when two tectonic plates abut and slide past one another. The interactions of the Pacific and North American plates over the last five to twenty five million years caused the volcanic upheavals and violent crustal deformities which led to the earliest development of the Baja California peninsula and the Sea of Cortez. The current configuration of the peninsula, the Gulf, and the islands has emerged only in the last five million years, a period of vigorous crustal subsidence and uplifting, as well as new sea-floor spreading. The western Gulf, the Baja peninsula, and a significant slice of the coast of California are still being rafted in a northwesterly direction by the counterclockwise rotation of the huge Pacific plate.

The Sea of Cortez is an extraordinarily rich area with a five-hundred-mile archipelago containing about fifty-five islands. There are basically two types of islands here: those that formed recently, in the last 10,000 years, and those that formed up to 4.5 million years ago. The important biological distinction between "old" and "young" islands rests in their relative lengths of isolation from the mainland populations of plants and animals, isolation which can lead to the development of unique or endemic life forms, where evolution has taken bold and sometimes strange directions. Not surprisingly, therefore, biologists often refer to islands as nature's own laboratories.

All of the major islands of the Sea of Cortez lie within the boundaries of the Sonoran Desert. The average yearly rainfall in the Gulf ranges from four inches in the midriff region to six inches in the south. In general, most of the rain occurs during the warm months of the year. The climate of the Gulf region is not as arid as the rainfall data would seem to indicate, however, as the island environments are modified by the surrounding sea.

I have chosen four islands for a cross-sectional survey of the entire Gulf. They are introduced in a north–south sequence. The first three fit into the "old" island category, whereas Islas Partida and Espíritu Santo are among the "young" islands. To enhance the scope of the story, different aspects of the natural, and in some cases unnatural, histories of each island are emphasized. The section on Isla San Esteban discusses native peoples, Isla San Pedro Mártir is about sea birds, endemism is explained in the description of Isla Santa Catalina, and geology is the

Page 80: Isla San Pedro Mártir
Page 82: Brown booby

central story on Islas Partida and Espíritu Santo.

Isla San Esteban is a small island, about four miles long and three and a half miles wide. Nevertheless, it climbs high above the surrounding sea to a height of 1,772 feet with much of its coastal edge terminating in bluffs of 100 to 500 feet. The island is composed of volcanic rock of Miocene age (more than twelve million years old), but its history as an island begins much more recently. When the Pacific tectonic plate peeled away the sliver of land now known as Baja California, the rock that would become Isla San Esteban was drawn far enough into the gulf to develop several endemic life forms as well as to support a unique human culture.

Early in the last century, a traveler might have witnessed a group of long-haired boys cavorting on one of the island's steep slopes. Their game was simple: On sleds made from discarded green sea turtle shells, who would dare to slide closest to the perilous drop at the island's edge? These boys were the hopeful future of the San Esteban Seri Indians. In reality, they would be their last generation.

The Seri Indians were hunter-gatherers who practiced no agriculture.[2] They lived in a fragile balance with a beautiful but harsh desert wilderness, where fresh water was a constant concern. The Seri were organized into several distinct bands that inhabited the coastal region of mainland Mexico in what is now the state of Sonora, and the two adjacent islands of Tiburón and San Esteban. The Seri who lived on San Esteban were thought to be the most primitive of the bands and they numbered no more than one hundred souls.

Their island is located in what is referred to as the midriff region of the Sea of Cortez, the narrowest part of the Gulf. Between stepping-stones of land, the greatest open sea distance from the Mexican mainland to the Baja peninsula is just over ten miles. The constriction here causes powerful tidal currents, as corroborated by the name of one of the islands and a major channel, Salsipuedes, or "Go if you can!" It is no wonder the San Esteban Indians were considered great seafarers by the other Seri, for they were known to put to sea under almost any conditions in their seemingly flimsy reed canoes. Across six miles of open and often dangerous waters, they would voyage to Isla Tiburón to augment their scarce supplies of fresh water.

Like the Miocene-aged rock upon which they lived, these Seri migrated into the Sea of Cortez. When they came is not known. We do know, however, the story of their end. Sometime in the mid nineteenth century, during a period of renewed conflict between the other groups of Seri and the Mexicans, the San Esteban Seri were annihilated. The Mexicans, who were engaged in ongoing skirmishes with the mainland Seri over their killing of livestock and their blatant acts of insurrection, were frustrated in their attempts to impose order. Never having understood the autonomy of the Seri bands, the Mexicans decided to strike at the Seri who were the easiest to find. They raided San Esteban and all of the Seri were rounded up in a single military sweep. The men were executed, the women and children sent to southern Mexico to work on plantations. Virtually all that is left of this Seri island culture is mysterious piles of stones and some broken pottery.

One of the best landing sites on San Esteban is in a protected bay at the south side. Above the beach is a broad but short arroyo with many large, isolated boulders. Overall, the island vegetation is very similar to that of the neighboring coast of Sonora, Mexico. The arroyos are dominated by deep-rooted trees and shrubs and the hillsides harbor fine growths of shallow-rooted, succulent agaves, ocotillos, and cacti, including the giant cardon. Throughout the arroyo are islands of vegetation dominated by several species of woody legume trees, such as mesquite, ironwood, and palo verde. The ground under these plants provides a more equable home for other, smaller plants because they moderate temperature, humidity, direct solar radiation, and, in some cases, increase the nitrogen content of the soil. Indeed, many of the smaller plants would not be able to grow in the absence of the large "nurse plants."

The Seri name for Isla San Esteban, *Coftécöl*, is derived from their word for the gigantic pinto chuckwalla, *Coof*, which is endemic to this island.

Pages 84–85: Displaying frigate birds, Los Islotes

83

On a hot spring or summer day these three- to four-pound vegetarian lizards come out in phenomenal numbers. It seems that a person can hardly walk one hundred feet in the arroyo without encountering a lizard sprawled within the branches of a shrub. Their huge bodies sometimes bend the entire plant close to the ground. At night and at colder times of the year the lizards retreat to shallow burrows under large boulders or into small caves which several lizards might share.

Based on a survey of the island's food resources, the San Esteban Seri must have had a high proportion of animal food in their diet. The most highly esteemed item on their menu was the East Pacific green turtle which abounded in the shallow waters around all of the midriff islands. The Seri Indians were aware of winter dormancy in these primarily vegetarian turtles long before it was brought to the attention of the scientific community in 1976.[3] During the winter, the sluggish turtles were easy prey for the Seri who hunted them with harpoons from their reed canoes. Unfortunately, for both the Seri and the sea turtles, Mexican fishermen, diving for abalone, also discovered the "sleeping" turtles around 1975. From then until 1980 (when they became too rare for commercial exploitation), the turtles were ruthlessly hunted by Mexican divers for the high price their meat would fetch. Despite recent conservation efforts their future is still uncertain. Like the Seri Indians of Isla San Esteban, the sea turtles, too, may perish.

Isla San Pedro Mártir juts abruptly from the sea. In the distance it appears as a single bluish-white rock, hundreds of feet high with smooth unscalable sides, and a thin white frosting. A perfect time to anchor offshore is in the cool hour before dawn, when a thick fog masks the island. A distant cacophony of barks, growls, whistles, and crashings echoes through the dense mist. Beyond the foggy bank, the boulder-strewn beaches and sheer cliffs break the vigorous flexing of this young sea. Atop and among the boulders, California sea lion bulls bark and growl their challenges. From the cliffs above a thousand birds call to their real or prospective mates. The air carries the strong, heavy odor of accumulated guano from millions of birds, past and present.

As the sun rises higher and the fog lifts, the ship is seen to be dwarfed by the towering mass of the island. The reflected glare of the early morning sun off the cliffs seems painfully bright as the astonished traveler strains to watch thousands of birds take to the air in search of food, mates, and nesting territories.

The ability to protect their young by nesting in trees, on cliffs, and on islands was one of the great evolutionary benefits birds gained by sacrificing their front legs and taking to the air. Every year these birds are able to make the journey to Isla San Pedro Mártir to nest in a mammal-free environment. Mammals have always been expert nest predators and many scientists have hypothesized that the dinosaurs were hurried to their ultimate extinction by the grizzly work of early mammals. It is probably more than coincidental that birds are the only surviving descendants of the dinosaurs.

Due to its great quantities of guano, lack of a permanent water source, age, and isolation, San Pedro Mártir has an extremely impoverished flora and fauna. There are only twenty-four recorded species of plants on the island. Of these, a dwarfed variety of cardon cactus dominates the landscape. The stocky grayish-green cactus stems form continuous ranks which are forever climbing up rocky arroyos and steep slopes. Most of the other plants are small, twisted, and inconspicuous, except for the large-leafed Palmer's fig which grows only at the top of the island. The number of native island animals is also scant. The vertebrates are represented by three species of reptiles, including a rattlesnake. Only the birds give an abundance of life to the island, a life which they both produce and support.

By late winter the blue-footed boobies begin to arrive in large numbers to stake out nesting territories, court, mate, and raise one or, occasionally, two chicks. Like their relatives on the Galapagos Islands, they nest on the ground and use no material to construct a nest; yet, in their courtship, the male ceremonially presents twigs to the female, an anachronistic behavior passed down from their nest-building ancestors. Their courtship dance is rich in symbolic gesture. The male and female walk in circles about each other, holding their blue feet out for inspection, pointing their beaks high into the air, and, sometimes, throwing their wings back and stretching their heads toward their partners. These newly betrothed couples share the island with other species of birds who have come here to nest as well—brown boobies, red-billed tropic-birds, Brandt's cormorants, and brown pelicans.

Around the island float great rafts of eared grebes, unable to fly until they grow back the feathers lost in their annual molt. When danger threatens, they dive beneath the water; danger always lurks. Avian predators come here to reap a harvest of defenseless eggs, chicks, and temporarily flightless birds. Over the island and along the shore move the ever vigilant yellow-footed gulls and black common ravens, waiting for a chance to dive in and snatch an unguarded egg or chick. High overhead soars a pair of rare peregrine falcons who occasionally make a successful strike on a distracted eared grebe. The eared grebes also suffer from the playfulness of the young sea lions who will repeatedly pull a bird under water until it drowns, and then leave the carcass of their discarded toy for a yellow-footed gull.

Probably the most unique year-round inhabitant of the island is Palmer's side-blotched lizard. The side-blotched lizards are excellent over-water colonists and they occur on almost every island in the Sea of Cortez. Those islands with the longest history of isolation host endemic species and subspecies. The side-blotched lizard on San Pedro Mártir is an endemic species. It is larger than normal, about eight inches from snout to tail tip. It is also an unusual monochromatic gray, perhaps a camouflage trick of nature which allows them to blend into the guano-dusted rocks upon which they perch. But their most striking adaptation is their strange relationship with the nesting birds.

The Palmer's side-blotched lizards have formed a volunteer sanitation corps for their own benefit. If a bird is clumsy or unlucky enough to have an egg broken, a lizard is there to lap up the mess. If the young chicks are sloppy and drop some of the fish brought to them by their parents, the volunteers dart in to clean it up. Each blue-footed booby nest seems to have one or more of the lizards in constant attendance.

Only two mammals have influenced the island: man and the rats he has introduced. Even today the descendants of rats who escaped from the ships of early explorers are reported to survive on the island. Other human influence has been more ephemeral. In pre-Columbian times, the island was probably visited by Indians who collected eggs and perhaps hunted sea lions, but there is no evidence of a settlement. San Pedro Mártir would be a difficult place to live due to its isolation, lack of water, and dearth of other food resources. The Mexicans continued the egg collecting and, in the late 1800s, established a settlement or penal colony for mining guano. In 1888 more than 135 Yaqui Indian guano miners were stationed on the island. Surviving on rations brought in by boat, they performed their unpleasant task under suffocating conditions of intense heat and nauseating odor. They existed in stone huts and these, together with the rock fills they built in every gully, remain as testimony to their miserable labors.

Today the island once again belongs to the birds. The ruined buildings have been appropriated by the nesting blue-footed boobies. Each year the birds continue to perform their strange dances and the air is still filled with their ceaseless calls and pungent odors. Isla San Pedro Mártir remains a window onto a bizarre and timeless world where man is an intruder.

From a distance, Santa Catalina has no features which distinguish it from most other islands in the region. Nor is there any evidence of the special magic it contains. It is about seven and a half miles long, running from north to south, and about two miles wide. The eastern edge of the island has high, steep slopes and a few narrow, rocky beaches. The chain of hills running the length of the island gently sweeps to the sea in the west. Even the highest peak, at 1,543 feet, is diminished against

Pages 88–89: Cardon cacti, Isla San Esteban

the profile of the nearby Sierra de la Gigante mountains on the Baja peninsula.

For the sunbather and shell collector the landing is a disappointment. The beach is narrow and cobbly. Whatever unlucky shells have been cast ashore are broken or ground into dust. Behind the beach a broad sandy arroyo snakes inland toward the island's eastern backbone. After a few minutes of walking, the sight, sound, and smell of the sea is gone. The even footing and soft sand make the arroyo easy to walk in, enabling one to look up and about rather than at one's feet for a safe footfall, and to see how the life of Isla Santa Catalina tells a story about adaptation and unique solutions to evolutionary problems.

The arroyo is bordered by steep, thickly vegetated slopes. Sentinellike, hundreds of large cacti loom above and protect the sanctity of the island. The cactus color-guard is composed of several species: galloping cactus, or pitaya agria, cardon, and the giant biznaga, or barrel cactus. While not an endemic species, this barrel cactus is a gigantic variety found only on Isla Santa Catalina.

Unlike the other large cacti, the four- to eight-foot-tall biznaga is not supported by a rigid wooden skeleton, but is held up by a tough rootstock anchored to the rocky soil, and a reticulated fibrous network underlying the skin. An adult plant, often unable to support over five hundred pounds of water-impregnated tissue, may crash over and die. This evolutionary "short-sightedness" does not apply to the smaller barrel cacti which do not require a strong support structure. Environmental and ecological conditions on Isla Catalina must have favored larger individuals, but why have they not, then, developed a skeleton, if this would ensure their evolutionary success? This is a question to speculate about while walking along the path of the arroyo, but there is a larger, and more fundamental, question which must be addressed: Why is it that islands harbor a relatively large number of unique plants and animals? This question has intrigued and excited naturalists for over a century. To consider it, we must first understand the relationship between evolution and islands.

There are fewer species of plants and animals on an island than are found in a comparable area of equal size on an adjacent mainland. This is due, in part, to the fact that there is a lesser diversity of habitats on an island than on a mainland. In addition, the total number of species on an island is a consequence of immigration rates, because the surrounding sea presents an inhospitable barrier to many species. It is easier for a bird, or a bird with a barrel cactus seed stuck to its foot, to fly to Isla Santa Catalina than it is for a spadefoot toad to swim to the island. It is also easier to emigrate to an island close to the mainland. As a result, Isla Santa Catalina, which is distant from the coasts, has only a fraction of the total number of species which reside on the adjacent mainland.

One of the species absent from Santa Catalina is the jackrabbit. Jackrabbits will frequently dig at the roots of barrel cacti in an attempt to reach the succulent tissue and avoid the sharp spines. The disturbance of soil, and the destruction of the roots which anchor a large barrel cactus, can cause it to fall over and eventually die. The absence of jackrabbits on Santa Catalina, by itself, might be enough to explain why the biznaga to grow to such a prodigious size. However, the ecology of the Isla Santa Catalina biznaga is the sum of numerous factors, many of which are yet unknown.

While walking ever deeper into the island, a small lizard is encountered dashing across the ground. As on Isla San Pedro Mártir, this ancient island has also spawned a remarkable variety of side-blotched lizards. Most desert lizards advertize sex and dominance with bright colors, which are usually kept hidden under the body until needed. The endemic side-blotched lizard of Santa Catalina has boldly cloaked its entire body in sexual pigments of bright greens and blues. This may be due to a dearth of predators with color vision, or perhaps this is some new scheme for cryptic coloration. Whatever the reason, the Santa Catalina lizard adds a special element of beauty to the island.

At the end of the day, with the sun low on the horizon, the broad rocky slopes of Isla Santa Catalina turn to gold. The air is cooler, and some of the more prudent animals become active. One of these is the endemic Santa Catalina rattlesnake. Coiled in the still warm gravel of the arroyo, the pink-tinged snake is easy to overlook. Although it is small for a rattlesnake, it has the characteristic morphology—triangular head, heavy body, thin neck, and the two extra holes in the snout. These holes lead to heat sensors which allow it to hunt warm-blooded prey on even the blackest nights. What makes this snake unique is that it has no rattles, just a single button! The rattleless rattlesnake is another example of what can happen on a small isolated island. In other parts of the western hemisphere, one in about every ten thousand births results in a rattlesnake which never grows rattles. On Isla Santa Catalina, where there are no large animals to step on the snake and where predators are almost unknown, this mutation was selected for and, over time, became "fixed" in the population.

As the last light from the sun disappears, the rising full moon can be followed from the top of the island. Its cool white light is reflected in a broad corridor on the calm surface of the Sea of Cortez. Eventually the moonlight reaches Santa Catalina. From up here, the spotlighted island looks dramatic and lonely.

Islas Partida and Espíritu Santo appear to be a single island of about twelve miles long and from two to five miles wide. In reality they are separated by a narrow channel navigable only by small craft. High, steep cliffs tower over the east coast while a series of tilting ridges and plateaus slope toward the western shore. The west coast has a barrier of low cliffs serrated by deep coves, the work of continuing rain and erosion which will eventually reduce these islands to a chain of the rocky crags feared by mariners and referred to simply as "foul water."

While well endowed with a diverse flora and fauna, the islands appear barren. Their most striking feature is their geology. Viewed from offshore, they look like a giant layer cake which has been carelessly dropped on the ground and kicked a few times.[4] Several bands of rock, sometimes tilted with the aspect of the islands, sometimes contorted at impossible angles, weave a simple pattern of surprising beauty. Highly reflective white strata are composed of compressed volcanic ash. Dark olive green strata are the result of hot molten lava rapidly cooled in an ancient sea. Many other colors and textures contribute to the aesthetic of this awesome primal sculpture.

The colonization of the islands by mainland plants and animals was facilitated by the last series of ice ages. The mile-thick ice fields, which crushed parts of North America, Asia, and Europe, contained tremendous quantities of water from the world's oceans. In the Sea of Cortez, the sea level was lowered by about three hundred feet and, until ten thousand years ago, it was possible to walk to Islas Partida and Espíritu Santo from the peninsula. This proximity has resulted in a relatively high species diversity and a low level of endemism.

On the west side of Isla Partida is a beautiful protected cove named Ensenada Grande. The slope of the white sandy beach is shallow and the water in the bay has an aquamarine cast. Smooth, reddish bluffs of compressed ash and cinder are honeycombed at the tideline with small caves. Behind the beach are sheer cliffs of stone overlooking a narrow, climbing arroyo that is choked with huge, sharp-edged boulders. The ground is difficult to traverse. The only easy places to walk are scoured areas in the arroyo which are dug into living rock. Nevertheless, the rich flora and fauna stubbornly thrive on the hard surface of the island. Isla Partida is vibrant with their colors, shapes, odors, and sounds. Palmer's fig trees cling to the cliffs and dig their white roots into cracks and gaping fissures. Delicate-leaved palo blanco trees dot the arroyo like banners at a medieval pageant. In the spring a riot of vines, such as coralvine, morning glory, coyote melon, spiny cucumber, and balloon vine, cover rocks, shrubs, and each other. Several species of giant cacti are visible everywhere. As is true throughout the Sonoran Desert, virtually all of the plants have some sort of defense to protect their precious hoards of water. The cacti and many other plants have thorns or spines. Others, soft and yielding, protect their water by mixing it with noxious volatile oils. Bruising their foliage

Pages 92–93: Dolphin skeleton

creates a strong and pungent odor, not rude or fetid, but rather an olfactory narcotic. One, the torchwood tree, was used by the Aztecs to scent the air of their dark temples for holy rituals. The Old World relatives of torchwood, frankincense and myrrh, were also highly valued for their aromatic properties.

There is an abundance of animal life on the islands. They are virtually overrun with a chocolate-colored variety of the black-tailed jackrabbit. Many of the giant cacti, especially the cardon, bear the scars of the rabbits' desperate gnawing. In areas where the rabbits are particularly abundant, some of the cardon cacti show a browse line where the stem has been eaten through to the skeleton. The caves in the cliffs are homes for great horned owls and ringtail cats. Costas' hummingbirds are frequently seen foraging on flowers or performing incredible aerobatics, such as mating displays. The distinctive call of the canyon wren issues from rocky crevices and floats down the arroyo. Bright orange, three-inch-long wasps with black wings visit the delicate white flowers of the palo blanco trees.

Pools of temporary water allow amphibians to live here. Two species of toads, Couch's spadefoot and the red-spot toad, probably arrived long before Partida and Espíritu Santo were islands. The toads spend most of their lives underground in a dormant state until the summer rains begin, when they leave their burrows to feed and reproduce. Both species have rapid rates of larval growth and development which allows the larvae to complete their life cycle in a small vernal pool. It takes as little as eight days for the egg of Couch's spadefoot to hatch, pass through the tadpole stage, and metamorphose into a small terrestrial toad. This is the most rapid developmental rate for any amphibian known.

Seasonal supplies of fresh water have also made it possible for people to inhabit the islands. When the Spaniards first arrived here during the sixteenth century, they found Indians who were willing to trade them pearls. The native islanders had long valued the black pearls which they harvested from the surrounding waters. Although these Indians left no survivors, clues to their culture can be found among the rocks: graves, paths, low stone shelters, grinding stones, hand tools, and piles of oyster shells. They were a stone-age people living in a garden of rocks.

Despite the oppressively hot summers, the scanty rainfall, and the isolation, life flourishes on the islands of the Sea of Cortez. Each generation produces new winners and losers for the natural selection sweepstakes, where success can lead to a new species and failure can mean extinction. Waves, wind, and rain still eat away at the islands and forces deep within the earth continue to build and shift the land. Even man has changed. No longer are any of the major islands called home, but each year they attract the scientific, the curious, the adventurous, and the romantic.

DENNIS CORNEJO

NOTES

1. The geologic history of Baja California and the Sea of Cortez is discussed in chapters 3 and 6 of *Island Biogeography of the Sea of Cortez*, T. J. Case and M. L. Cody, eds. (Berkeley: University of California Press, 1983). This is also the best source for plant and animal lists for the islands.

2. The history and culture of the Seri Indians as well as their use of plants and animals is beautifully documented in Richard Stephen Felger and Mary Beck Moser, *People of the Desert and Sea: Ethnobotany of the Seri Indians* (Tucson: University of Arizona Press, 1985). There are still Seri living in Sonora, Mexico. I frequently use the past tense when talking about them because, culturally, they are not the same people I describe in the text.

3. For more information on the East Pacific green sea turtle in Mexico see R. S. Felger, K. Clifton and P. J. Regal, "Winter dormancy in Sea Turtles: Independent Discovery and Exploitation in the Gulf of California by Two Local Cultures," *Science* 191:283–85, and K. Clifton, D. O. Cornejo and R. S. Felger, "Sea Turtles of the Pacific Coast of Mexico," in *Biology and Conservation of Sea Turtles*, K. Bjorndal, ed. (Washington, D.C.: Smithsonian Institution Press, 1982), pp. 199–209.

4. This is with apologies to Joseph Krutch who also described the island as a layer cake. However, I had written the description before reading his book; it is still the best way to visualize the islands! Krutch also provides a wealth of information on these islands in his book *The Forgotten Peninsula* (Tucson: University of Arizona Press, 1961).

Page 95: upper left, Pacific rattlesnake; upper right, Hermit crab; middle left, Desert spiny lizard; middle right, Monarch butterflies; lower left, Red-billed tropicbird, Isla San Pedro Mártir; lower right, Black jackrabbit, Isla Espíritu Santo

Page 106: Blue-footed booby, Isla San Pedro Mártir
Page 107: Living stromatolites, Isla Angel de la Guarda

Page 108: Giant barrel cacti, two generations,
Isla Santa Catalina
Page 109: Cardon cactus, detail
Pages 110–111: Los Islotes

An
Ungentled
Land

Evidence of the past in Baja California is fresh—it has not yet been obliterated by civilization's freeways, building projects, and trash. The mountainous desert peninsula is a resistant land: some parts of it are little explored; other areas have rejected men and their settlements. Testimony to their efforts to prosper, however, is scattered about Baja California, reminders of man's fragile dreams. Exquisite cave paintings, ruins of adobe walls and old stone churches, rusted mining machinery and gaping shafts, all are monuments to the men and women who have struggled in this arid and harsh wilderness.

Caves and shelters hidden in Baja California's most inaccessible mountains belonged to the painters of prehistory. In steep-walled canyons, beside quiet pools of cold, clear water, Indians of centuries ago painted murals of heroic men and beasts in the ochre, sooty black, and burnt red tones of the earth. In overhangs, in slit caves, and on seemingly inaccessible walls, powerful representations of deer, serpents, fish, and human figures splash the creamy rock. Questions of who these painters were and when they lived abound. What is certain is that the cave art was painted long before the first Europeans found the tip of Baja California in the early sixteenth century, by a people who had vanished centuries before.

Baja California was discovered by Europeans in 1533. Ordoño Jiménez, who came upon the peninsula, was a mutineer aboard one of Hernándo Cortéz's ships. After murdering the captain of *La Concepción*, he navigated her into the Gulf waters

and put in at La Paz. When his sailors appropriated some of the Indian women of the area, Jiménez and twenty of his crew were killed. Thus Jiménez has the double distinction of discovering California and being among the first Europeans to die there.

At the time of its discovery, the peninsula was inhabited by at least forty thousand Indians belonging to three main groups: Pericues in the Cape region, Guiracuras from La Paz to Loreto, and Cochimes to the north. These were further divided into subgroups, each with distinct dialects. All were hunters and gatherers. Their technology was simple, as was their material culture. Bows and arrows, spears and fish nets, woven bags and baskets were the tools of their subsistence. Log rafts, reed flutes, and feather blankets were other possessions noted by the Jesuit missionaries who arrived in 1697. The men walked naked while the women wore brief string skirts made from agave fiber. Edward Cooke, an officer with Woodes Rogers, the Bristol privateer, said the Indians of Cabo San Lucas, which they visited in 1709, were scrupulously honest and very hospitable, and excellent swimmers and divers.[1] Jesuit Padre Johann Baegert, who lived in Baja California between 1750 and 1768, noted that the Indians "are well-shaped and well-proportioned people, very supple ...with very few exceptions, they all walk perfectly upright, even when they are far advanced in age. Their children stand on their feet and walk before they are a year old. Some are tall and stately, others small of stature, as elsewhere, but none

Page 112: Canada de la Candelaris, Sierra de San Francisco
Page 114: Spanish mission church, San Ignacio

among them is conspicuously fat, the cause of which may be that they do much running and walking and therefore have not time in which to fatten."[2]

The Indians lived in small nomadic groups and occupied temporary brush shelters, or, occasionally, caves. Their diet was as varied as the natural resources. Seafood was the staple along the coast and birds, reptiles, insects, and rodents provided protein for those who lived inland. Because water was scarce, settlements concentrated where natural springs promised permanent supplies. These would later become mission sites. The organ-pipe cactus, or pitahaya dulce, provided abundant and delicious fruit and was so highly esteemed that the Indians' only calculation of time was based on the pitahaya season. When pitahayas were ripe, the Indians wandered from tree to tree, gorging themselves and becoming so fat that, Baegert declared, he did not recognize some of his own parishioners when they returned from months of feasting.[3]

Cortéz himself occupied the peninsula in 1535, establishing a colony at La Paz, which he called Santa Cruz. In his explorations, he found a bay near Cabo San Lucas which came to be called California, a name taken from the contemporary romantic adventure novel, *The Exploits of Esplandian*, in which it said, "On the right hand of the Indies there is an island called California, very near the terrestrial paradise—an island peopled by Amazons."[4] The name *California* was later applied to the whole peninsula, Baja (Lower) California, as well to the land to the north, Alta California.

After two disheartening years on the peninsula, Cortéz returned to Mexico, but he commissioned Francisco Ulloa to explore further. In 1539 Ulloa sailed to the head of the Gulf of California, which he named *Mar de Cortéz*. He established that California was a peninsula, as cartographers were to depict it through the sixteenth century. Ulloa pushed up the west coast of the peninsula to Cedros Island, where he arrived on September 9, 1540. He sent a ship back to Mexico with a progress report for Cortéz, then sailed northward, never to be heard from again.

There were other voyages of exploration and attempts to colonize the peninsula by the crown or individuals, all with motives of profit. Little gold was found in Baja California, but there were black pearls and local Indians were pressed into service in the sporadic pearl fishery around La Paz, nicknamed La Perla.

For a century and a half, Baja California remained without a permanent European colony or installation, demonstrating the peninsula's disappointing yields and its resistance to exploration and settlement. In the meantime, Spain's conquest of the Philippine Islands gave her access to the riches of the Orient and control of the Pacific.

In 1566 a merchant galleon crossed from Acapulco to Manila, returning with a cargo of silk, tea, porcelain, and gold. This became an annual voyage, each year seeing a great ship sailing westward, carrying from four to six hundred passengers, and returning early the following year laden with treasure. The voyages were long and difficult, with crew and passengers victims of scurvy, but they were very profitable. While the logistics of this annual voyage were problem enough, it was at least made somewhat safer for the first thirteen years because Spain had control of the Pacific. Then, in 1578, that control was broken when the English corsair Francis Drake came through the Straits of Magellan and coasted northward, raiding and despoiling. In 1579 he captured the Peruvian galleon *Cacafuego* off Panama and stole its heavy cargo of silver. Finally, he sailed past Baja California and, after resting near Point Reyes, sailed on westward around the world to anchor at Plymouth on September 26, 1580.

In 1587 another young corsair, Thomas Cavendish, followed Drake's path into the Pacific, raiding the coastal towns and ships of New Spain. He repaired his vessels near Mazatlan, then sailed to Cabo San Lucas to wait nearly a month for his prize, the Manila galleon *Santa Ana*. The great ship was defenseless and easily taken, yielding an enormous treasure of gold, silks, brocades, perfumes, and pearls, the greatest loss sustained by the Manila galleons in their two hundred fifty years of

Pages 116–117: Friar Rocks, Cabo San Lucas

service. Cavendish put the surviving passengers ashore and burned the *Santa Ana*, then sailed on to raid the Philippines, finally reaching Plymouth in September 1588 to mark Elizabethan England's second circumnavigation of the globe in eight years. Spain's complacency was shattered and her Pacific realm was no longer secure.

The loss of the *Santa Ana* made the need for protection more urgent. In 1602 Sebastián Vizcaíno was sent to find a port on the Pacific coast where the ship from Manila could seek refuge; he failed. However, a Carmelite friar in his company, Fray Antonio de la Ascensión, erroneously reported that California was an island with a strait north of Cape Mendocino, connecting the Pacific Ocean with the Sea of Cortéz. The mistake was repeated on maps and charts for the next century.

It was missionary zeal, not conquistadors or treasure seekers, that finally conquered California. On October 15, 1697, a small band of Jesuit missionaries led by Juan María Salvatierra landed on the peninsula near present-day Loreto. They came with the authority of the viceroy to undertake the conversion of California on the condition that it be at the order's own expense, and that the land be possessed in the name of the King of Spain. Father Salvatierra's authority extended to temporal matters, both military and civil. The California mission was small, under one hundred souls for the first few years, but it was powerful. Along with the missionaries came attendant servants, soldiers, and their wives, a group that was to form the core of a distinctive social element in the Baja California of the future, the Californios.

The Jesuits were superior missionaries, well educated and trained, excellent administrators and builders, and their accomplishments during their seventy-year occupation of Baja California were remarkable. In a land without skilled artisans, timber, or essential building materials, they constructed eighteen missions. Yet on February 3, 1768, Carlos III, the Bourbon King of Spain, expelled the order. The founding of the missions and conversion of the peninsula were accomplished by a total of thirty priests and two lay brothers, half of whom remained buried in Baja California when the Jesuit community departed.

Franciscans, under their president, Father Junipero Serra, were ordered to take over the Jesuit missions, although their authority extended only to religious affairs. The crown, however, desired a Spanish presence in Alta California to thwart the new colonizing efforts of England and Russia. It sent Captain Gaspar de Portola, Governor of California, on an overland expedition with Serra to found missions in San Diego and Monterey.

The Dominican Fathers of Spain also wanted a stake in California and, in 1768, King Carlos III decreed that some missions be given to them. The Dominicans arrived in 1773 and controlled the peninsular missions for the next half century, extending their claim northward to their last mission at San Miguel, halfway between Ensenada and San Diego.

Father Serra was delighted to hand over the entire peninsula to the Dominicans in exchange for exclusive rights to the more fertile lands from San Diego north.

Although now romanticized, the mission period was an unhappy and unfortunate time for the Indians. Missions were established at sites with permanent water sources, which was also where the nomadic hunters and gatherers naturally congregated. The Indians were easily subjugated and forced to labor, building huge adobe or stone churches, dams, and irrigation systems for the mission estates. The Padres' standards of morality were rigorous and discipline was harsh. Most devastating of all were the waves of epidemics which swept the land one after the other. Because the indigenous populations possessed no natural immunities and were housed in overcrowded conditions at the missions, disease spread like brushfire. Smallpox, measles, typhoid fever, malaria, typhus, and syphilis, introduced on the cape by the soldiers and sailors from passing ships, decimated populations. The burial record for Mission Santa Gertrudis, for example, shows five epidemics in thirty-five years reducing the population from seventeen hundred to three hundred. According to current estimates, during an eighty-year span, the indigenous population declined from forty thousand at the time of the first permanent white settlement to about five thousand in 1777.

By the early 1800s the mission system had collapsed. The dismal failure of the missionary process was not due to an inability to convert the Indians but rather to the rapid disappearance of Indians to convert. Only at San Ignacio was there a resident priest after 1808. One hundred years later Arthur North would write in *American Anthropologist*, "The end of the Baja California Indians is near at hand."[5] Today they are extinct.

There is another indigenous people of Baja California, however, which still exists as a regional subculture, the Californios. These ranchers—some would say the last true cowboys—are descended from the soldiers, sailors, and servants brought by the missionaries to assist in religious and military endeavors. Hundreds of families live in the remote reaches of the sierras which run along the spine of the peninsula, in the steep granite terrain virtually untouched by the modern day. They live as did their ancestors, raising their herds of cattle, riding horseback, tending their orchards and vegetable gardens just as the missionaries of nearly three centuries ago. They dry and prepare meat, and tan hides to tool them into saddles, chaps, and a variety of leather goods. Each family has its shrine, for they are Catholics—not by conversion, of course, but by heritage.

Mexican independence, declared in September 1813, did not help Baja California and its people. There were more than fifty rulers of Mexico in the next sixty years, including presidents, dictators, and emperors. Local politicians gave the church lands to friends and supporters. In 1846, following the annexation of Texas in 1845, President James K. Polk declared war against the Republic of Mexico with the intention of annexing Alta California. American troops were also sent to Baja California, where they occupied all of the main towns and were repulsed only at Muleje.

As was the case in Alta California, many of the leading Mexican families felt they would be better off under the American flag, due in part to its government's greater stability, and volunteered allegiance to the United States. There was little difficulty in taking the peninsula with such a supportive citizenry. However, the Treaty of Guadalupe Hidalgo, signed on February 2, 1848, gave Alta California to the United States and returned Baja California to Mexico.

American interference in Baja Californian affairs was not over. In 1853 an American filibuster, William Walker, attempted to establish a "Republic of Sonora and Lower California." Sailing from San Francisco with a modest force of adventurers, he took La Paz, proclaimed the republic, and hoisted a two-star flag. Walker's forces were later defeated in northern Baja California.

Relations between Mexico and the United States improved after that. In 1870 Mexico allowed the United States Navy to maintain coaling stations for its Pacific fleet at Pichilingue Bay near La Paz and in Magdalena Bay. In 1873 and 1885 the United States ships *Hassler* and *Narragansett*, at the request of the Mexican Government, conducted hydrographic and biological surveys of the coastline of the peninsula and its adjacent islands. Their marine charts are still used today.

In an attempt to promote colonization, the Mexican Government granted enormous concessions to private American and English companies between 1880 and 1889. In 1884 American Major George Sisson and Luis Huller, a Mexican citizen, were granted almost all of the peninsula, to exploit the minerals and fisheries, and to sponsor agricultural development. This concession was purchased in 1885 by the International Company of Mexico, based in Hartford, Connecticut, for a substantial amount. In 1887 Ensenada was developed by an English corporation called the Lower California Land Association and three hundred colonists, mostly from England, settled there. In 1890 the Lower California Development Company, another English concern, bought one hundred thousand hectares at San Quintin, dredged the harbor, built a railroad, a flour mill, hotel, and a telegraph line to Ensenada, and instituted weekly steamer

Pages 120–121: Cemetery, San Ignacio

service to San Diego. Trial wheat plantings had produced an abundant harvest in 1889, an unusually wet year. When normal drought conditions returned, however, the English colonists' crops and orchards withered.

All of the concessions were doomed to failure. In 1917 President Venustiano Carranza canceled most of the foreign concessions and, in 1933, the last of them were repossessed by President Abelardo Rodríguez. The existence of the grants was considered generally detrimental to the development of the peninsula as a whole, Ensenada being a possible exception.

Exploitation of natural resources was the principal interest of foreigners in Baja California. The pearl fishery was to continue until 1936, when it was wiped out by a mysterious disease which attacked the pearl oysters. Manganese was mined for the United States, at Magdalena Bay during World War I, and Conception Bay during World War II. One of the great copper mines of the world, El Boleo at Santa Rosalía, was long worked by a French company. Between 1914 and 1918 twelve German square-rigged, coke-supplying vessels were caught there, trapped by British and American naval vessels. Their crews suffered because France and Germany were at war, and the French mining company refused to release necessary food supplies. During the delay, German sailors became acquainted with the Mexican señoritas and made substantial contributions to the gene pool.

Natural resources are still exploited by foreign companies. There are enormous salt works at Guerrero Negro, developed by the American shipping magnate Daniel Ludwig, with salt evaporating ponds in Scammon's Lagoon now replacing the worked-out fossil salt beds. Barges transport the salt to a deep-water transshipping facility on Cedros Island, where it is reloaded into huge bulk carriers. The south and west sides of San Marcos Island have immense deposits of very pure gypsum which have been developed by Kaiser Permanente, an Oakland company, which supplies gypsum all over the world.

It was along the northern border that the American connection was to be most important. The taming of the Colorado River required Mexico's cooperation and, at the same time, insured Baja California of a dependable supply of irrigation water on its side of the border. The Southern Pacific Railroad joined Baja California with mainland Mexico in addition to the United States, the two markets for its agricultural products. Still, many of the huge farms developed on the Mexican side of the Imperial Valley were owned and operated by Americans.

In 1920 Prohibition was enacted in the United States. This resulted in the greatest boom Baja California had yet experienced. The border villages of Tijuana and Mexicali provided liquor and other tourist attractions, and the rush was on. Baja California received undreamed-of tax revenues which allowed General Abelardo Rodríguez, who became Governor in October 1923, to build schools and highways, and even for Baja California to lend funds to the Federal Government. General Rodríguez was Governor through 1929, then was made interim President of Mexico in 1932. As President he declared Mexicali, Tijuana, and Ensenada free ports, a status most recently renewed in 1983.

Tourism remains Baja California's largest industry. The trans-peninsular highway, airlines, and cruise ships bring American visitors in phenomenal numbers. Luxury hotels line the beaches of Baja California's Riviera, from Cabo San Lucas to La Paz. Millions of visitors venture just across the border to enjoy Tijuana, Ensenada, and Mexicali. San Ysidro, the American port of entry opposite Tijuana, is said to be the most heavily traveled border crossing in the world.

A traveler to the midriff area of the peninsula on the Gulf is likely to meet many fascinating people, but none is more impressive than Antero Díaz, the jovial and hospitable patriarch of Bahía des los Angeles, a village nestled at the base of a tall mountain on the edge of the beautiful island-studded bay of the same name. Antero's erect carriage and quickness of mind belie his more than seventy years, fifty spent as Bahía's leading citizen. He is a man upon whom many depend for their very living. To me, as to a multitude of Americans, he is known as Papa Díaz, and his wife, Cruz, as Mama Díaz, of Bahía.

Antero arrived from central Mexico in 1940 and went to work for an American mine investor at the little gold-rush settlement of Bahía de los Angeles, actually just three or four adobe houses and a dozen tents and shacks for prospectors who had responded to rumors of a new gold discovery near some old diggings. The gold fever soon faded and the prospectors drifted off, but Antero and his young family stayed.

Bahía de los Angeles had a dependable supply of fresh water in the form of a spring that had been used by Indians for six thousand years. It also was near the sea's resources. Antero utilized both. Green turtles were abundant, and were harvested by his fishermen and trucked alive to market in Tijuana and San Diego. The distance was only a little more than four hundred miles but took four days over the bone-shattering road. The turtle-laden trucks crept north, and returned with drums of fuel and other supplies from the border.

Soon, American tourists, the first of a hardy, adventurous lot, began to bump their way over the tortuous trail to Bahía de los Angeles. Antero's blacksmith and mechanic repaired the battered cars and Mama Díaz prepared green turtle steaks. Papa Díaz's hospitality gradually became legend.

Sport fishing boats made their appearance in the fleet and the paddles and sails of the turtle fishermen's dugout canoes were replaced by outboard engines and fiberglass hulls. Antero built a gravel airstrip and Bahía de los Angeles became a destination for adventurous fliers who could land and taxi their little aircraft right to their rooms.

The Diazes' energy and labor brought prosperity to Bahía de los Angeles. Antero constructed a school in the village and arranged for a teacher. He built a cement-block church for the village, too, with colored glass in the steel-framed windows, but that was against the law and soldiers came from Ensenada and dynamited it. So Antero built a better church on his own property. Everyone is welcome to pray there.

Today, Bahía de los Angeles has a jet airstrip, immigration and customs officers, a Captain of the Port, a military base, a fish and game office, several motels, service stations, and stores, a water desalinization plant, and electricity twenty-four hours a day. There is even a research station to study and protect sea turtles. A paved highway connects Bahía de los Angeles with San Diego to the north and La Paz and Cabo San Lucas to the south.

Antero and Cruz have witnessed development and change, and are responsible for much of it. Papa and Mama Díaz are distinguished Baja Californians, benefactors of the country in which they live. To his neighbors at Bahia de los Angeles, Papa Díaz is Don Antero, and that is as it should be.

Baja California has been discovered, and some small parts of it may have been spoiled for those who knew them earlier. On the whole, however, the peninsula remains a beautiful, wild, natural place. There are still mountain ranges and islands where no people live. There undoubtedly are ancient cave paintings not yet discovered. The traditional and natural courtesy and hospitality of the *rancheros* is as strong and genuine as ever. Now much of the peninsula can be visited and enjoyed in comfort or even luxury. But vast areas, still protected by their isolation, are waiting to be enjoyed by intrepid explorers.

GEORGE LINDSAY

NOTES

1. Captain Edward Cooke, *A Voyage to the South Sea and Round the World, Performed in the Years 1708, 1710, and 1711* (London: B. Lintot and R. Gosling, 1712).

2. Johann Jakob Baegert, *Observations in Lower California*, translated from the German with introduction and notes by M. M. Brandenburg and Carl L. Baumann (Berkeley: University of California Press, 1952), p. 53.

3. Ibid., p. 35.

4. Pablo Martinez, *A History of Lower California*, translated from the Spanish by Ethel Duffy Turner (Mexico 14, D.F.: Editorial Baja California, 1960), p. 90.

5. Joseph Wood Krutch, *The Forgotten Peninsula* (Tucson: University of Arizona Press, 1961, 1986), p. 116.

Page 124: Spanish mission church, San Ignacio
Page 125: Mission San Borjas

Pages 126–129: Natural stone sculptures, Cabo San Lucas

Page 130 (above): Baja California rock art detail
Pages 130–131: Mural in Gardner Cave

Page 132: Rancheros curing leather
Page 133: Details of handtooled saddles

The
Whale
Lagoons

For most of its eight-hundred-mile length, the Pacific slope of Baja California is officially desert. It is not the desert of our imagination, with endless expanses of barren sand stretching to the horizon, but desert by definition, a land with less than ten inches of annual rainfall, generally high temperatures, and an evaporation rate considerably higher than that of the precipitation.

As do most deserts it supports a highly specialized plant community and an assemblage of animals adapted in intricate and fascinating ways to live successfully under extremes of heat and aridity. They tend to be small, cryptically colored, and inconspicuous.

Here and there along this low, barren-looking coast, great lagoons have formed, transforming the landscape. It is to these sheltered waters that a great number of gray whales come annually to bear their young.

About 350 miles south of the United States–Mexican border, the Sierra Vizcaíno de San Andreas advances into the sea, forming Punta Eugenia, the most prominent geographical feature of the entire coast. The submerged mountain range reemerges offshore as Isla Cedros and, even farther out, as the Islas San Benito. Together the cape and islands bound a vast bay, Bahia Sebastián Vizcaíno, and one of the largest lagoon systems of the continent has developed where the head of the bay inundates an extensive shallow plain.

The conditions here were right for the growth of a barrier beach: abundant sand, a gently sloping foundation, and steady wave action on an exposed

coast. These conditions have prevailed for at least the last 1,800 years so that, today, the barrier is nearly two miles wide in places. The lagoon is closed from the sea except for three inlets that still flush it with the rising and falling of each tide.[1]

Each flood tide brings more sediment from the sea to be deposited near the head of the lagoon where water movement is slight. The shallows become shallower, a process aided by wind-driven sand streaming in from the barrier beach and its dunes. At the upper edge of the shallows, salt-tolerant plants take hold and the process of sediment buildup accelerates until a land bridge is finally formed.

These processes have succeeded in cutting what was a single, giant lagoon of two hundred square miles into three, Manuela, Guerrero Negro, and Ojo de Liebre (also known as Scammon's Lagoon), each with its own sea link. These inlets open into relatively narrow channels that shoal and spread as they near the head of the lagoon. Twice a year, during the solstices, spring tides carry salt-rich sea water far beyond the head of the lagoon into a series of shallow pans where it gradually evaporates, producing salt flats. In 1957 this process was exploited commercially and over nine million tons of salt have been produced to date.

San Ignacio Lagoon, about one hundred miles south of Punta Eugenia, is the best known of the whale lagoons thanks to the research of biologists studying the California gray whale. The lagoon is a system of relatively deep channels surrounded by

Page 144: Spy hopping California gray whale, Laguna San Ignacio

Page 146: Sand dollar on Isla Magdalena

extensive intertidal flats winding sixteen miles into the desert. Its wide entrance, marked by an endless parade of breakers, funnels into these protected channels where the gray whale cows come to bear their calves.

One hundred miles farther south lies the third major lagoon system, totally different in architecture. At its southern extremity, its barrier island is anchored on the mountainous Isla Magdalena. Because it is enclosed by islands rather than by a barrier reef of sand, it is officially a bay, Bahía Magdalena. Broad and shallow, it extends parallel to the coast for thirty miles before joining the lagoon proper through a narrow, tortuous canal, flanked at low tide by broad sandbars. Behind these flats where shore birds, herons, and ibis feed, a mangrove forest has established itself.

Santo Domingo Lagoon is a narrow ribbon of water emerging from Bahía Magdalena and paralleling the coast northward for ninety miles. The barrier is breached by three inlets, Boca de Soledad, Boca Santo Domingo, and Boca de las Animas. The seaward face of each barrier is a superb beach of surf-packed sand, pavement-hard. They are places for walking alone, for letting the wind and surf and sand work their magic. The vistas seem endless.

They are a beachcomber's heaven. Jetsam from passing ships and even from the cities of California may find its way here but natural flotsam predominates. Shell treasures, figs, the giant Ferguson cone, diminutive hatchet shells by the thousands, and an astounding variety of bivalves abound, each showing their strange adaptations for living successfully in shifting sand. Sometimes a fish, a sea turtle, or even a dolphin lies half buried at the tideline. These edible treasures account for a tracery of coyote tracks along the drift line and the occasional scrutiny from a low-flying turkey vulture or raven.

Birds are few on these hard sand beaches, as the pickings are lean; a lone reddish egret may search the wave wash and a small company of sanderlings may drift like flying spume, chasing the margin of each wave across the sand. But inside the lagoon there is an explosion of life. The lagoons are oases of vitality in an otherwise parched and still landscape.

Between November and February you will find up to ninety thousand brant, about half the population of the eastern Pacific.[2] This energetic little sea goose is one of the greatest fliers of all the geese. Its nesting grounds stretch from Wrangell Island, Siberia, to the central coast of the Northwest Territories of Canada. Each year in early autumn the brant from all parts of this vast summer range converge upon Izembeck Lagoon on the Alaskan Peninsula, there to fatten for their great test of fitness. By late October they are physiologically ready and need only the stimulus of appropriate weather. When, in November, the wind flow is right, the geese rise several thousand feet into the night sky and the entire population sets a direct overseas course toward the lagoons and bays of Baja California some three thousand miles to the southeast.[3]

They will stay here for three months of feeding and rest. Then the gradually lengthening spring days trigger the pituitary hormones and, once again, stir these restless little geese to migration.

As they leave the opulent lagoon environment they seem more relaxed than when they arrived. They depart in small groups and tarry frequently on their long journey, to feed, court, and ready themselves for the rigors of the nesting season to come.

The warm salty waters of the lagoons are richly productive, every incoming tide bringing a new influx of oxygen and nutrients to maintain the lagoon organisms. The waters become a soup of minute floating plants and animals that contribute, in turn, to an abundance of invertebrates and fishes. They are a magnet to birds of many species who feel the call of the lagoons when winter draws its blind across the northern part of the North American continent.

From the rangelands of British Columbia the long-billed curlews lead their young southward to join the marbled godwits, avocets, and willets that have nested about the lakes of the Great Plains.

Pages 148–149: Avocets and willets, Magdalena Bay

Sanderlings and dunlins come in from the arctic coast, long-billed dowitchers and western sandpipers from the shores of the Bering Sea. Surf scoters from the Yukon muster for the winter along with other wading birds and waterfowl from the north. Overshadowed by the throngs of migrants, the resident brown and white pelicans, white ibis, and as many as six species of herons and egrets must share the same resources.

In San Ignacio Lagoon two islands, Isla Garzas and Isla Pelicano, offer nesting colonies of sea birds protection from coyotes, foxes, and other ground predators. Garzas reportedly supports the greatest density of nesting ospreys known, 130 pairs, along with dozens of brown pelicans, reddish egrets, and double-crested cormorants. A pair of peregrine falcons is reported to nest on the island, well nourished by hordes of shore birds and ducks.

Despite this lavish display of birds, the great attraction of the lagoons is really the gray whales. Nowhere else in the world are there as many of a single species of great whales concentrated in such a small area. In any one of the three major lagoons, Ojo de Liebre, San Ignacio, and the Bahía Magdalena complex, from early January until well into April, whales will be present.

It is estimated that there are fifteen thousand gray whales in the world today. Every year around eleven thousand of them swim from the Bering Sea to the coast of Baja California, a round trip of more than ten thousand miles. This is the longest migration of any mammal in the world.

In late summer the gray whales that have spread across the shallows of the Bering Sea begin to swim southward. Led by the heavily pregnant cows they enter Bristol Bay, pass the entrance to Izembeck Lagoon, where the brant are beginning to gather, and reenter the North Pacific via Unimak Pass. The first wave of migrating grays passes northern British Columbia in early December, swimming steadily at about four knots night and day, navigating we know not how. By early January they have reached their goal, crossed the bar at the entrance of their chosen lagoon, and entered the warm, protected shallows within. From then until spring the main area of the lagoons is occupied primarily by pregnant females and cow-calf pairs.

The great body of the migration is strung out for hundreds of miles but the lead swimmers reach the coast of Baja California in January and, in the words of one whale researcher, "In the breakers, over the sandbars, in the channels and the nearby open ocean the water is full of whales."[4]

Some cows don't quite reach the lagoons and new-born calves have been seen as far north as southern California. Most of the calves, however, are born in and about the lagoons in late January and early February. By mid-February cow-calf pairs are everywhere in the lagoons; the new-borns, about fourteen and a half feet long, shadow their mothers, surfacing and diving in time with her movements.

The intimate details of the lives of the great whales are hidden from us and it is seldom we get even a glimpse of the moment of birth. However, Storro-Patterson, in 1977, by an extraordinary combination of skill and luck, watched this critical episode in the life of a new-born whale. He writes: "The calf I observed surfaced and breathed several times on its own, without any assistance from the cow. The cow actually swam rapidly away from the calf at the moment of birth. After thrashing and tail lobbing for a few minutes, she returned and lifted the calf out of the water. She repeated this a few times during the next several minutes. The calf seemed very awkward and even desperate at times. It would lurch at the surface, appearing to be trying to lift itself out of the water. . . . The calf inhaled water a few times, only to lunge and struggle more energetically at the surface. . . . Within a period of approximately 30 minutes following birth the calf calmed down, surfacing and breathing in a coordinated way."[5]

Several hundred people a year now make the pilgrimage to the lagoons to associate with the gray whales. In small boats they move carefully and quietly into their vicinity. Early in the season the cows are usually protective of their new calves and keep their distance from the boats. By February, however, they are more relaxed and the calves seem curious about the world they live in. Some of these small whales, sometimes both mother and calf, will approach the boat.

The phenomenon of "friendly" whales was reported first at San Ignacio in 1978 and now is known to include both young and old individuals. It is an unforgettable experience to have a forty-foot gray whale, scarred by generations of barnacles and the misadventures of thirty or forty years at sea, bring her month-old calf to the side of your fragile craft.

Next to this experience, the grisly events of just a century and a half ago are unbelievable. In these same lagoons American whalers brutally slaughtered the gray whales for their oil, bringing them close to extinction.

Whaling captain Charles M. Scammon, for whom one of these lagoons was named, gives a vivid description of the methods and perils of whaling in the Baja lagoons. "A cow with a young calf is usually selected so that the parent animal is easily struck . . . the murderous blow [with the harpoon] often causes the animal to recoil in its anguish and give a swoop with its ponderous flukes, or a toss of its head, which, coming in contact with the boat, produces a general wreck and more or less injury to the men. In the winter of 1856 we were whaling about the esteros of Magdalena Bay, where, in attacking sixteen whales, two boats were entirely destroyed, while others were staved fifteen times, and out of eighteen men who officered and manned them, six were badly jarred, one had both legs broken, another three ribs fractured, and still another was so injured internally that he was unable to perform duty during the rest of the voyage."[6]

Later he wrote: "None of the species [of whales] are so constantly and variously pursued as the gray whale; and the large bays and lagoons, where these animals once concentrated, brought forth and nurtured their young, are already nearly deserted. The mammoth bones of the California gray whale lie bleaching on the shores of those silvery waters and are scattered along the broken coast from Siberia to the Gulf of California; and ere long

it may be questioned whether this mammal will not be numbered among the extinct species of the Pacific."[7]

Now, after forty years of protection, the gray whale has rebounded in numbers to near its original population. The shifting sands have removed without trace the bleaching bones and the shattered fragments of the ships lost in the pursuit of the whales. The new generation of whales seems to carry no memory of the experience of their ancestors at the hands of man and has no fear of people who come gently to observe and marvel. This is one of the very few success stories in whale conservation.

The quietude of life in the inner sanctum of the lagoons contrasts with the circus of mating activity in the sea beyond. Vigorous chases are frequent as the bulls seek mates. Tail lobbing, breaching, rolling, and thrashing the surface are all part of the courtship. As bulls outnumber receptive cows, trios are frequent, and a cow will have two bulls each trying to mate with her. The love-making of a pair of forty-foot whales is of stupendous proportions.

Then the bulls leave. By February most of them are on their way northward. Indeed, there is traffic in both directions through much of the winter; the late southers off California pass the early northers already answering the call of the Bering Sea.

The cows and calves linger, but by late February every ebb tide sees another movement into the open sea. The calves show great excitement as they meet the cold sea water and feel for the first time the thrust of the surf surging across the bar. They breach, lunge, and spy hop as they leave their birthplace and pass out to meet the adventures of their first migration. The last cows are gone by May, hugging the shoreline and skirting the kelp beds as they take the route north on which they are least likely to encounter the predatory orca.

The vibrant life within the lagoon inevitably preempts attention to the point that it is a relief to the senses to turn away from the water and to experience instead the tranquility of the dunes. Wave upon wave, the dunes, sometimes over

Page 152–153: California gray whales Magdalena Bay

twenty feet high, advance from the ocean barrier beach toward the lagoon itself. The steady wind drives sand grains up the gradual slope on the windward side to the crest. A few moment's inspection of the downwind face will reveal that sand is constantly cascading in small sand avalanches. And so the dune moves steadily away from the wind at an average rate of two inches per day, or fifty-eight feet a year. Thus, in the passage of centuries, the dunes advance across the landscape, filling the shallows and spilling into the deep lagoon channels where an equilibrium exists and tidal flow removes the sand seaward to begin again its assault on the lagoon. Where there is a pause in the sand, specially adapted plants take hold: grasses, sand verbena, devil's claw, euphorbia, and other sand-loving species, and then a harsh, low shrubbery of salt bush that accumulates and holds the sand.[8]

In the full heat of day the dunes appear lifeless, but walk slowly across them in the early morning. Dewfall has dampened the surface and stilled the restless grains, creating a sand table that retains indelibly the signs of every passing creature. The complicated twin tracks of a wandering june beetle may intersect the equally distinctive tracks of a night-hunting lizard and cease. The dot-and-dash tracks of a jackrabbit moving between clumps of vegetation, the single line dimples of a trotting fox, or the pugmarks of a coyote reveal the story of the hunt. Tiny highways used by kangaroo rats or pocket mice in their endless search for seed; the single row of four-toed tracks left by a foraging horned lark or mourning dove can be seen on any dawn walk across the dunes. This sand landscape is a complete and ever-changing ecosystem, an essential element in the spectacular whale lagoons of Baja California.

IAN McTAGGART-COWAN

NOTES
1. F. E. Phleger and G. C. Ewing, ''Sedimentology and Oceanography of Coastal Lagoons in Baja California, Mexico,'' Geological Society of America, Bulletin no. 73:145–82.
2. A. S. Leopold, *Wildlife of Mexico* (Berkeley: University of California Press, 1959).
3. R. S. Palmer, *Handbook of North American Birds*, vol. II (New Haven: Yale University Press, 1976).
4. R. Storro-Patterson, ''Biological Aspects of the Eastern Pacific Stock of the Gray Whale,'' *Eschristius Robustus* (background papers for workshop on international cooperation for conservation of gray whales, I.U.C.N.).
5. R. Storro-Patterson, ''Biological Aspects,'' pp. 1–65.
6. C. M. Scammon, *The Marine Mammals of the Northwest Coast of North America*. (New York: Dover, 1968), pp. 258–61.
7. C. M. Scammon, *Marine Mammals*, p. 33.
8. W. Inwan, ''Coastal Sand Dunes of Guerrero Negro, Baja California, Mexico,'' Geological Society of America, Bulletin no. 77:787–802.

Page 155: Osprey and coyote

Page 156: California gray whale breaching

Page 157: upper, Laguna Ojo de Liebre;
lower, California gray whales, mother and calf

In the Lap of the Ocean

Any island, approached for the first time, presents an exciting new world to explore. Not even an experienced biologist can predict what might be discovered on one. Islands are laboratories of evolution, too. Their isolation from new genes and their small founding populations provide the seeds for evolutionary change.

Many islands are born when a sinking coastline, or a rising sea, inundates a peninsula and leaves a high seaward area isolated. These islands, termed *continental*, occur with a built-in complement of plants and animals. As if on a grounded ark, everything that lived on the end of the peninsula when the seas cut it off is now an inhabitant of an isolated island.

Many organisms are present in such small numbers that the population soon disappears. Other species cannot meet all their needs within the confines of the island, or experience one of the outbreaks of disease that no species can escape, and die. The larger and more specialized creatures are most vulnerable. Those that prey for a living are especially at risk. No island, for long, retains all the life forms it was born with but, in general, the larger the island and the more varied the habitats on it, the greater the variety of life it can support.

Some islands arise out of the sea through volcanic eruption or another geomorphic process and thus come into being without terrestrial plants or animals of any kind; these are called oceanic islands. They do not remain pristine for very long. Plant seeds arrive on the wind, on the wave, or car-

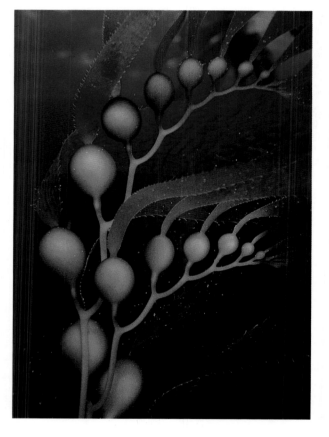

ried by birds. Insects and spiders also may ride the winds to this new land. Lizards, good colonizers, come by raft on floating logs or clumps of debris washed off the beach from some far-away continent. Birds arrive on the wing, when they are blown off course during migration or hurled out to sea by hurricane winds.

Mammals, on the whole, are poor colonizers of islands. If unfortunate enough to be carried off by a rising tide, few could survive the long period at sea without food and water. A notable exception are the seals who actually need and seek an island's isolation for the successful reproduction of their species.

The Pacific coast of Baja California boasts nearly a dozen islands of varying origin and size. Most interesting to the biologist and, indeed, to the nature lover are Islas Cedros, San Benito, and Guadalupe.

Isla Cedros lies off the hook of Baja's west coast, about halfway down its length. Twenty-four miles in a north–south direction, with a rugged backbone of mountains rising sheer from the surf of its western shore, it carries several peaks approaching three thousand feet in altitude. Cedros is in the coastal fog belt and, though its rainfall is meager, its high peaks are cooled and moistened by the fog and support a forest of pines and junipers, the "cedars" that gave it its name.

As the sea closed its circle around Cedros, sluicing away the sea-level sediments, it sorted blocks, boulders, cobbles, gravel, and sand into a complex of shoreline habitats. Each was quickly colonized

Page 158: Isla Guadalupe
Page 160: Kelp

by the fascinating assemblage of shallow-sea organisms whose spores and larvae float in every wave. Seaweeds, green, brown, and red, in threads, sheets, or globules settled on the naked boulders alongside the newly attached barnacles. Segmented worms, long and slender or short and bristled, hydroids, brittle stars, and sea cucumbers sheltered under stones; sea urchins, crustaceans of bewildering variety, sea hares, bubble snails, beautifully camouflaged chitons, limpets, cowries, and abalones quickly colonized the new habitat with a host of other creatures.

Each habitat gained its complement of fish, from the diminutive goby peering out of an abandoned worm tube to the sharks ceaselessly patrolling in search of prey.

The seals discovered Cedros, a protected beachhead, to bear their pups. No doubt, the fast-moving, exploratory California sea lions were the first to come. With hind flippers rotated forward, they scrambled quickly up the beach or even clambered up the steep faces of rocky headlands. Soon, thousands of them occupied most of the suitable habitat. By 1965 it was estimated that 8,400 sea lions lived on Cedros while the number at sea was unknown.[1]

The northern elephant seal, giant of the Pacific seals, is a pioneering species with a proven ability to occupy new range quickly. Unable to use their hind flippers for walking, the great creatures undulate clumsily on their bellies over sand or gravel beaches.

In late December and early January, the coves and beaches gradually fill with the great beasts, rolling fat from months of rich feeding in the deep offshore waters. They arrive one by one, the relatively svelte cows up to ten feet in length and weighing one thousand pounds or more, the bulls twice that length and weighing up to two tons. With frequent pauses to rest muscles that have not been used for many months, they heave themselves above the tideline where the cows relax, spaced by their intolerance.

The huge senior bulls, the beach masters, fifteen or more years old, begin their contests for position and status. Massive heads reared high on ponderous necks, proboscides inflated and arcing into cavernous mouths, they challenge. A measured, reverberating series of guttural claps rolls along the beach, clearly audible above the pounding surf and the bedlam around the cows and pups.

Bull threats are settled by striking down at the adversary's neck from a full height of five feet or more. Deep wounds are torn, even in the callused neck armor of the great contenders. Eyes may be gouged, proboscides lacerated, and canines broken before the loser retreats with the winner in pursuit.

The sooty-black pups are born between December and March. They weigh in at about forty pounds and immediately set about the urgent task of nursing on the mother's extremely rich milk. Growth is phenomenal. During the average nursing period of twenty-seven days, the pup gains about 160 pounds.[2]

When weaned, the pups are deserted by their mothers. Alone, they cluster together and watch the world with oversized black eyes that will stand them in good stead for hunting in the dim light of the deep sea. They pass hours in sleep, idly scooping sand onto their backs in the heat of the day and, infrequently, wandering to the water's edge. But mostly this is a resting time, as their load of baby fat is slowly used to fuel the important physiological changes that will fit this young land creature to cope with the perils and opportunities of the ocean. Without teaching or example, each must learn to be an elephant seal, to go where the food is, to dive for, hunt, and capture the great variety of fish and squid it uses, and to avoid the predatory great white shark and orca; and, five years or more into the future, to find its way back to the breeding beaches of Cedros to propagate its species.

By late March the beaches of Cedros are inhabited by dozens of sleek pups, a smattering of sub-adults, and a few exhausted bulls, shrunken, scarred, and battered from three months of fasting, fighting, and breeding. They lie like hulks, sleeping until the urge to lumber down the beach, sink into the cool ocean water, and turn northward for months of incessant feeding to rebuild their

Pages 162–163: California northern elephant seals hauled out, Isla Cedros

strength and energy stores for yet another year returns.

Isla Cedros has a rich flora featuring six plant associations: pine forest, juniper woodland, chaparral, coastal sage scrub, seashore dune scrub, and desert scrub.[3] Fifteen of the island's plant species are endemic, plants that evolved here and have their entire population confined to this small universe.

But a terse classification of this remarkable assemblage of plants does not do justice to their variety, color, form, and texture. From the somber pines that crown the mountains to the delicate ferns that cling to the creviced walls of narrow canyons, Cedros is a botanical delight. The most spectacular plant is certainly Shaw's agave with its towering eight-foot flower stem crowned with masses of golden flowers, each containing a flask of nectar that draws a variety of winged creatures.

From its continental past Cedros inherited brush rabbits, pocket mice, white-footed mice, wood rats, and black-tailed deer. All have been isolated for so long that they have evolved into subspecies or species unique to this island. The Cedros mule deer is noteworthy not only for its distinctive features of color and skeleton, but also for its status as the only endangered race of black-tailed deer in the world. Perhaps as many as one hundred of these small deer cling to existence among the pines at the north end of the island. If at one time there were coyotes, foxes, or ring-tailed cats on the island, today predators are absent.

Two dozen species of birds, most of them residents, have been reported on the island as well as twelve kinds of reptiles. That three of these are found only on Cedros is testimony to the effectiveness of the water barrier and the millennia through which the island has been a haven for small landbound creatures.

The Indian inhabitants of Cedros were removed from the island by Spanish missionaries more than 250 years ago but modern man has returned. At the island's south end is a thriving small port town based largely on fishing and on transshipping the salt barged over from Laguna Guerrero Negro.

Tucked into a sheltered bay toward the northeast corner of the island is a small cluster of brightly painted buildings, homes of the families of several fishermen. Their small open boats, as brightly colored as their houses, ride at anchor in the bay. Each is equipped with an air compressor and two coils of air hose, the gear divers refer to as a hooka. Using this equipment, the men scour the rocky bottom for the abalone and spiny lobsters that are the basis of their livelihood.

Twenty-four miles farther out to sea the Sierra Vizcaíno de San Andreas merges again as the three small islands of San Benito. Apparently oceanic in origin, these volcanic islands support their own mini-mountains, the tallest of which is 660 feet in height. Parched and treeless, the islands are nonetheless quite well vegetated thanks to the frequent fog and dew that supplement the rains. Cholla and mammillaria cactus mingle with thickets of cliff spurge and other drought-toughened shrubs that stand leafless through most of the year. The winter rains transform the landscape. Cacti swell with moisture and send out buds; the numerous rosettes of agave expend the energy of decades in one reckless display of golden flowers. Everywhere, dormant seeds of annuals germinate and grow to flowering in precipitate haste. Brodeas top their nodding stems with clusters of mauve bells. The spurge leafs out and covers itself with tiny cream blooms and the flamboyant San Benito mallow unfolds its large white-and-purple flowers. Even a few plants of the indigenous Dudleya have escaped the grazing burros to send up their flower spikes.

The instinct to select nesting sites on well isolated islands has been crucial to the success of many species of oceanic birds. Several have taken advantage of the remote Islas San Benito. Western gulls and brown pelicans are on their nests in March and April. Elsewhere on the flats, where deeper soils have collected, and on selected hillsides, the burrows of Cassin's auklets, Xantus' murrelets, and black and least storm-petrels are numerous. By day only a small mound of loose earth at the burrow entrance, the prints of small webbed feet, or a splash of white excrement tell of the presence of this avian night shift. But anchor in the bay at night, with lights ablaze, and the hurrying shapes of these diminutive sea birds will be seen as they shuttle between sea and shore. Occasionally, confused by the lights, one will land on the deck and permit a more intimate view.

A small fishing village, quite similar to the one on Cedros, has been a feature of the western end of San Benito for many years. Until recently, there was also a manned lighthouse on the western cape. With people came their hangers-on: burros, dogs, and cats. The burros have changed the vegetation by selectively consuming the more palatable species. Their damage is widespread. Cats and dogs are a hazard to the nesting sea birds.

One hundred sixty miles to the northwest, the most isolated of all the islands of the Pacific coast of Baja California rises four thousand feet from the sea. Isla Guadalupe is obviously oceanic in origin, the volcanic cap of a great mountain rising twelve thousand feet from the sea bed. Twenty-two miles long and three to seven miles wide, Guadalupe is cliff-girt with few nooks that permit landing from the sea.

It was the globe-girdling whalers and sealers who first explored the island in the early 1800s, although it had been known for nearly 250 years by that time. The seal hunters found thousands of fur seals among the boulders and in the deep shoreline caves. The wealth to be gained from the seals' glossy pelts drew men year after year from halfway around the world.

When first seen, this spectacular island was described as a naturalist's paradise. Today it is one of the most thoroughly devastated islands in the world.[4] The sealers built stone huts ashore and, year after year, returned to slaughter the seals until, by 1830, there were not enough animals left to justify the journey. This small remaining number increased in time, and a second assault occurred between 1876 and 1894. It was believed that the last individuals had been killed and that the species was extinct.

Then the elephant seals came under attack for their valuable oil and a herd of about fifteen thousand individuals was quickly brought to the vanishing point. In 1892 only nine animals could be found. But there were probably some young at sea that returned in later years to the empty breeding beaches and, unknown to the exploiters, bore their young. Mexican and American biologists searched the shores of Guadalupe in 1922 and counted 264 seals. The Mexican Government declared the island a refuge and stationed a party of soldiers on it to enforce the edict. The response of the elephant seals was immediate and spectacular. Not only did they recolonize the beaches of Guadalupe, but they slowly spread to the other islands so that, by 1977, it was estimated that the population was about sixty thousand individuals distributed over almost all of their original range from Isla Natividad, Baja California, to the Farallon Islands of California. This is one of conservation's great success stories.[6]

The southern fur seal proved less resilient. The tiny handful of survivors that escaped the clubs and guns of sealers has grown to about one thousand individuals but all are still confined to Guadalupe.

The seal slaughter was only a small part of the havoc man wreaked on this "naturalist's paradise." The sealers or whalers introduced goats to the island, and the damage these animals have done is unbelievable. They have eaten everything. The forests of pines, oaks, cypress, and junipers have been devastated. Many of the thirty species of endemic plants survive only on a small satellite island or in cliff crannies not reached by the goats. Because of the destruction of the natural habitat, of the nine species of birds endemic to the island, only four survive.

Baja California's other Pacific islands are continental in origin and hug the mainland shore. Even so, their natural life speaks for their isolation as well as for their limited potential as habitats. Los Coronados, the most northerly island group, has just three species of land mammals but hosts large colonies of pelicans, cormorants, western gulls, and Xantus' murrelets. Islas Todos Santos, San Martín, San Geronimo, Natividad—delightfully euphonious names, rich in Spanish history—are

Pages 166–167: California sea lions

all small and arid but nonetheless interesting. There are several plants unique to one or the other of the islands and each has at least one kind of small animal, some of them distinct subspecies.

Far to the south, Isla Magdalena and Santa Margarita bound the seaward shores of the Bahia Magdalena complex. They are large islands, strung out for many miles north and south, and are so close to the mainland that isolation is negligible. As a consequence, there is a greater variety of resident mammals. These two islands also display some of the most elegant sand dunes of the entire coast as well as mile upon mile of beaches of hard-packed sand that are a joy to the soul as well as a lesson in dynamic geography.

It is hard to imagine a dozen islands anywhere in the world that are more varied in origin, environment, flora, and fauna and that have been more intimately tied to the activities of man as depredator and conservator. Thankfully, today man's hand rests lightly on these fascinating places.

IAN McTAGGART-COWAN

NOTES

1. D. W. Rice, K. W. Kenyon and D. Lluch, "Pinniped Populations at Islas Guadalupe, San Benito and Cedros, Baja California in 1965," *San Diego Society of Natural History* no. 14, vol. 7:73–84.

2. B. J. Le Boeuf, "The Elephant Seal," in *Problems in Management of Locally Abundant Wild Mammals*, P. Jewell, ed. (Orlando: Academic Press, 1981), pp. 291–301.

3. D. L. Bostic, *A Natural History Guide to the Pacific Coast and North Central Baja California and Adjacent Islands* (San Diego, 1975).

4. L. M. Huey, "Guadalupe Island: An Object Lesson in Man Caused Devastation," *Science* no. 61:405.

5. B. J. Le Boeuf, "The Elephant Seal," pp. 291–301.

Page 169: Sand dunes, Isla Magdalena

Page 176: upper, kelp rock fish; lower, Garibaldi fish
Page 177: Great white shark

SELECTED BIBLIOGRAPHY

Brusca, Richard C. *Common Intertidal Invertebrates of the Gulf of California*. Tucson: University of Arizona Press, 1981.

Case, Ted, ed. *Island Biogeography of the Sea of Cortez*. Berkeley: University of California Press, 1983.

Crosby, Harry W. *The Cave Paintings of Baja California*. La Jolla: Copley Book, 1984.

————. *Last of the Californios*. La Jolla: Copley Book, 1981.

Gardner, Erle Stanley. *Off the Beaten Track in Baja*. New York: William Morrow, 1967.

Gotshall, Daniel. *Marine Animals of Baja California*. Ventura: Western Marine Enterprises, 1982.

Johnson, William Weber. *Baja California*. Alexandria, Va.: Time-Life Books, 1972.

Krutch, Joseph Wood. *The Forgotten Peninsula*. Tucson: University of Arizona Press, 1961.

Lewis, Leland R. *Baja Sea Guide*. Newport Beach: Sea Publications, 1971.

McGinnies, William, Bram Goldman, and Patricia Paylore, eds. *Discovering the Desert*. Tucson: University of Arizona Press, 1981.

Nabhan, Gary Paul. *Gathering the Desert*. Tucson: University of Arizona Press, 1985.

Peterson, Roger Tory, and Edward Chalif. *Field Guide to the Mexican Birds and Adjacent Central America*. Boston: Houghton Mifflin, 1973.

Shreve, Forrest, and Ira Wiggins. *Vegetation and Flora of the Sonoran Desert*. Stanford: Stanford University Press, 1964.

Steinbeck, John, and E. F. Ricketts. *Log from the Sea of Cortez*. New York: Viking Press, 1951.

Thompson, Donald, L. T. Findlay, and A. N. Kerstitch. *Reef Fishes of the Sea of Cortez*. Tucson: University of Arizona Press, 1979.

Zwinger, Ann. *A Desert Country Near the Sea*. Tucson: University of Arizona Press, 1983.

ABOUT THE CONTRIBUTORS

Lisa Lindblad was trained as an anthropologist and has written on a variety of subjects for *Intrepid* magazine. She is also the mother of two sons.

George Lindsay is a biologist and Director Emeritus of the California Academy of Sciences. His interest in the history and natural history of Baja California has been life-long.

Ian McTaggart-Cowan began his professional career as a biologist and served successively as Professor of Zoology, head of the Department of Zoology, and Dean of the Faculty of Graduate Studies at the University of British Columbia. He was the founding chairman of the Academic Council of British Columbia, and currently serves on a number of international and national councils concerned with scientific research and conservation of natural resources.

Dennis Cornejo has spent the last twelve years traveling and doing research in the Sea of Cortez. He has written on the area for various scientific and popular publications, on subjects including desert toads, sea turtles, botany, and the Seri Indians. He is currently working on a Ph.D. in botany at the University of Texas.

Sven-Olof Lindblad is a photographer and travel executive whose photographs have appeared in a number of publications, including *Signature, Gourmet,* and *National Geographic* magazines. He is president of Special Expeditions, Inc., which for several years has offered voyages in Baja California.